THE LANGUAGE OF DRUMMING BOOK

A System for Musical Expression

BENNY GREB

Written by Benny Greb

Edited by Joe Bergamini

Book Design by Rick Gratton and Benny Greb

Layout by Rick Gratton

Music Engraving by Willie Rose and Rick Gratton

Cover Design and Book Illustrations/Sketches by Tom Mayer, San Diego, CA

Executive Producers: Rob Wallis and Paul Siegel

CD Recording, Programming, Mixing, and Mastering by Benny Greb

"Grebfruit" Drum Solo Transcription : Mark Eeftens

Catalog: HDBK31/HL321287
ISBN: 9781458422293

HUDSON MUSIC®

In This Book

The Language of Drumming
INTRODUCTION

Welcome to this book. We have a fantastic journey ahead of us.

This book will not only enable you to play differently, but (more importantly) to think differently, and get a better understanding of rhythm. With the systems contained in this book, you could write a million more books. This material will give you the freedom to decode a lot of the other educational material out there, and (even more importantly) by having that ability, you will be free to come up with your own exercises, and have more freedom to make choices on the spot while playing music.

Why? Because we will work with the DNA of rhythm. You will find the ideas and concepts in this book present in all the music that surrounds you, and you'll see through things that were a mystery to you before. That's why the information here is timeless.

The system and principles I present in this book were part of music even before the drumset was invented, and I believe they will remain core principles of music for many, many years to come. This book is not restricted to a specific style of music or a way of playing. It will help you to widen yor perspective of rhythm and will benefit your playing no matter what you are working on at the moment.

The Goal

When I was six years old and started to play the drums, I already had a clear vision of what I wanted. I wanted to be able to play whatever I wanted, whenever I wanted, in any dynamic, and at any tempo. Well, at that age, when I referred to dynamic, I meant as loud as possible, and when I talked about tempo, I meant, of course, lightning speed. But with experience, I also realized the power and beauty of quiet, whispering sounds and slow tempos. By adding these extremes to the spectrum, we really have the definition of total freedom to express yourself on the instrument as a goal. And I always thought—and still do—that's a very good goal to have.

Needless to say, I'm not quite to the point where I can play "whatever I want, whenever I want," and so on, but I've made a lot of progress since then, and I'm working on it more efficiently than ever—and in this book I will share with you how.

The Inspiration

From the beginning, there were two things that fascinated me most about music.

The first is how music makes me feel; how it communicates feelings. Think about a film score. Sometimes you don't really hear the music—you just feel it. If you watch the same scene without the music, much of the mood and emotion is lost.

The second thing is how beautiful it was (and is) to watch great musicians play—and it seems to me that "playing" is the perfect word. How they seem to be able to have a complete musical conversation with little or no effort. I wanted to be inside the music and to feel it like them. I didn't want to have to think at all—especially not about where to put my hands or feet, and at what time. I wanted to have my playing at a level like talking: not having to think about how to shape my mouth or how to first put the words together before saying something, but feeling something and just saying it—without thinking about technique.

I started to play the drums without any system. I picked up certain things here and there: a two-bar rock groove with a suitable fill, and so on. Standard things that I was told should work. But when it came to expressing myself and interacting with musicians, I often felt very limited. I thought I needed even more standards. I tried to broaden my vocabulary, which was a good idea, but I still didn't have an overview of what the options were—again, because I didn't have a system. And I often had the same problems over and over.

The only way to solve a problem like this, no matter what the subject, is to understand how the whole thing basically works. If you understand the principles behind what you are trying to do, only then will you come up with solutions yourself. And I think we can use a metaphor from another field that all of us already use naturally: language.

Learning the Language

I'm from Germany. English is not my first language. I began to learn English like a lot of people first learn a new language. I learned a few phrases, like "Can you tell me the way to the train station?", or "Two coffees, please." (These should get you through London, even if you don't have a clue.) It was like learning a handful of licks for a certain musical style that "always fit"—but in music and language there are no licks that always fit. When I lived in the U.S.A. for a half-year when I was twelve, I learned quickly that I wasn't able to communicate with other people in this way, because they didn't answer like the examples in the phrasebook.

I understood that I had to learn the language the proper way from the very beginning: learning the letters (thankfully they are the same as the German ones), putting them together into words, making sentences, and slowly gaining the ability to have a conversation. It was easier and way more efficient than I expected, and it enabled me to eventually express myself freely in both German and English. Most importantly, I am not restricted to talking at people (like with the "lick" approach, where I prepare something in order to fire it off later) but communicate with people. Isn't that also what music should do?

So why don't we approach drumming the same way, since the drum was the earliest tool for communication? And to do that, we need the alphabet of rhythm.

I tried to find a system that includes every rhythmic phrase, figure, pattern—everything that appears rhythmically on this planet. I wanted to collect them all, write them down, and practice them: the millions of little components of which all the music around us is made. Totally thrilled about the utopia of my enterprise, I analyzed countless pieces of classical music, funk, rock, pop, and jazz—but along the way I came to the conclusion that there are not millions of little musical components. In my concept there are 24 of them.

So here we are.

If you really want to express yourself and be creative as a musician, don't try to find shortcuts. That will get you nowhere. This book shouldn't give you any "can-you-tell-me-the-way-to-the-train-station" kind of licks (although you can get many licks out of it, if that's what you're after).

My hope really is to give you a vocabulary, and ways to use it, so you can say what YOU want to say in the language of drumming.

Benny Greb

DRUM KEY

How To Use This Book

HOW TO...

1. Don't just play the through exercises, but also read the text. (Like you are doing now. Great! Continue...) The text holds keys to create much more material than is actually notated on the pages. Especially in the last chapters, there are some footnotes that include clues to how a new principle or variation can be applied to transform other exercises in the book. If all these other variations were written out, this book would have been ten times its current size. Through these hints, I was able to strip down the page count without throwing out a single idea. Be sure to give these footnotes a try, because they will make you feel like you suddenly have a *Language of Drumming Book 2* in your hands.

2. Although this book is full of notation, I don't want you to merely consume. When you are through with one page, instead of going on with the next one, I want you to stop for a second and think some very important thoughts that separate the good player from the great. Here are some examples:

> *"What is the essence of this?"*
> *"What would I do with this?"*
> *"What else can I do with this?"*

3. Expanding on this concept: Because we use a print medium here, what mostly gets translated is the *what*—the *what to play* for this or that exercise. But music happens largely in the *how* you play it. This is what I actually love about books. We get a lot of information, but the true character of the *how* is up to us. So it is your choice, and really a matter of your personal quality standard, if you manage to turn the exercises on these pages into something that has groove, dynamics, and all the other parameters that make up good music. So, broaden your perspective. When you realize you're focused on a certain technique, step back, play it again, and also listen to how it sounds. Or when you're looking at stick height and listening to your dynamics, also remind yourself about your body posture. This is what will help you to get the most out of this material, and it will turn you into your own best teacher.

When you analyze your playing, ask yourself: "How can I do this better?" "How did it feel?"

Always remember: Practicing an exercise until it sounds good is a low standard. We have to practice until it feels good (and then you'll realize it sounds even better!).

4. I think I already covered this, but just to make sure: Please note that on most of the exercises that feature drumset applications always show a basic ostinato to showcase a possible environment for the ideas. However, I kept these ostinatos very basic, so it gives the reader a quick entry to the exercise, as well as a clear, uncluttered appearance notation-wise. Please don't stop there. These are merely suggestions to get you started and inspire different ideas to come to life.

5. Also, on the pages that contain exercises, you will find boxes that let you write down the date and tempo as you practice. I know that when you really work with this book and make progress, there won't be enough space in these boxes. If so, then use an extra page, or, even better, write a practice diary. However you do it, I recommend you document your practice—so maybe look at those boxes as more of a constant reminder to do so.

...USE...

Actually use it! Use all of it!

I know this might sound simple, but it has a huge impact.

Did you know that of all the books sold worldwide, about 90% of them are not read past the first chapter? What a waste, right? I guess if we did a survey including drum books we would find even lower numbers. Do you own a drum book that you never worked through? Some exercises you never even tried? Some text you've never read? I know you do. You are not alone—I do. First of all, it's hard to really stay at it, and there also can be this psychological effect: "I own this book" equals "So now I *have* this material."

The bad news is we don't have anything unless it is really a part of us—unless we really do it, and do it repeatedly. A habit. Our musical capabilities are habits, and habits take quite some time to develop. And it gets even worse! Sometimes you'll work on something and think, "Oh yeah, I've got this," and then when you want to access the same stuff a month later, there's a huge question mark above your head. Almost anything gets unlearned when it is not practiced regularly.

The point I want to make is this: Really make use of all of the ideas in this book, and keep them fresh. The fact that you've read this already tells me that you are different. Well done. I now invite you to get the most out of this book by taking *what* is in here and putting your *how* to it.

...THIS BOOK...

is yours. Now make the content truly yours.

How To Use The CD

On the CD you'll find some practice tracks that can be divided into four categories. (Track list is on page 93.)

Guide Tracks:
These should be more than a "demonstration" of an exercise, but provide a nice backing track for practicing different incarnations of the alphabet, words, or syntax—no matter if it's just clapping the rhythms, or using it as a guide for rudiments or drumset applications.

Call and Response:
On each of these tracks, you will hear rhythms for you to repeat. This is basically a review/test to see if you can play and feel all the material in the corresponding chapter. It will also challenge your focus and your ability to listen and react quickly—one of the most important things for us musicians! Again, after you are through with the rhythms themselves, immediately use them to test your agility for the more advanced applications.

Jam Track:
Here a bass guitar will play along with you.

Warm-up to Burnout:
This is basically the alphabet a few times in a row, but every time it repeats, the tempo is 10 bpm faster. In the fourth bar of every letter you will also hear a rim click that plays what is about to follow. This way you don't have to memorize the alphabet to get through this. These tracks are useful as a reference that guides you through the alphabet in different tempos. They should also be applied to every incarnation of the letters in this book.

One version might be great for you to focus on accuracy while going through the rudiments and/or as a bass drum part. Another version might be perfect for a workout with singles on the right hand. Whatever you use it for, it will make the alphabet audible with a click in such a way that you can find out which incarnation of the alphabet is playable for you, up to what tempo. You can use this at first to to train accuracy with the click, then continue until you get to a tempo that pushes you to your maximum speed, until you have to drop out. Whatever you do with it, it's just there to give you a wide range of tempos for a wide range of different applications. For some exercises, some tempos feel very slow, but for others, the very same tempo makes perfect sense. I recommend you making full use of this phenomenon and really getting to know your repertoire in this way.

Have fun with this great tool. It honestly helped me a lot.

CHAPTER 1: *Letters*

Part A - WARM-UP

Letters
INTRODUCTION

A letter is the smallest element of Latin-descent languages. Of course we can make other noises with our voice, but to be a letter it takes more than just a noise: it's a short sound which contains information so that it will have a specific meaning when combined with other letters.

When I just hit the drum, it doesn't necessarily mean anything. It's how the sounds are organized—the context—that provides the meaning. This context consists of a rhythm's relation to time/the quarter-note pulse and it's subdivisions. VERY IMPORTANT: You have to make sure that you always feel/know where the quarter note is. It's not only important for the exercises to sound right; they must also feel right.

This is what I call the Rhythmic Alphabet. Together they are the 24 patterns I promised you earlier. The vast majority of what appears rhythmically in the music around us is derived of these elements. These are the puzzle pieces of every rhythmic picture.

Warm-Up/Clap Exercise: I call this chapter "warm-up" because you don't need good technique or a drumset for these exercises. You can practice them anywhere. You don't even need sticks! But actually this is way more than a warm-up. It's a mental workout that is the basis of all following exercises, so check it out.

Let's take a look at these letters. The binary letters shown here, A-P, have four possible spaces in which a note could be played. The dots in these diagrams represent a note that is played, while a dash represents silence or space between the notes. First we have the four possible one-note letters, followed by those with two notes, three notes, and finally all four notes.

The same applies to the ternary system (Q-X). Here we have all the possible permutations of three notes or rests on one beat.

Once you understand the basic rhythmic alphabet, we can then add some of the elements that we need to create music:

- **Tempo/Quarter-Note Pulse**

- **Subdivision**

- **Instrumentation**

- **Form**

The Rhythmic Alphabet

BINARY LETTERS

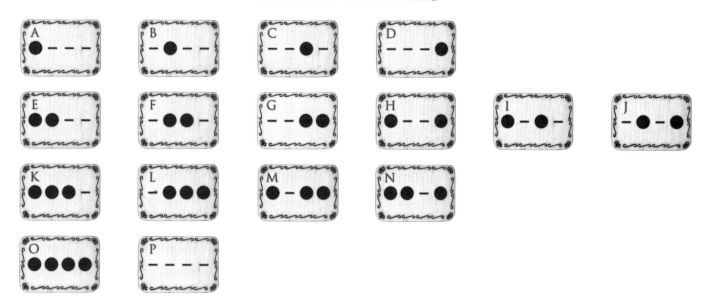

TERNARY LETTERS

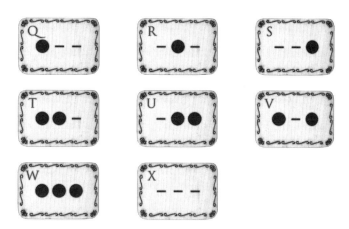

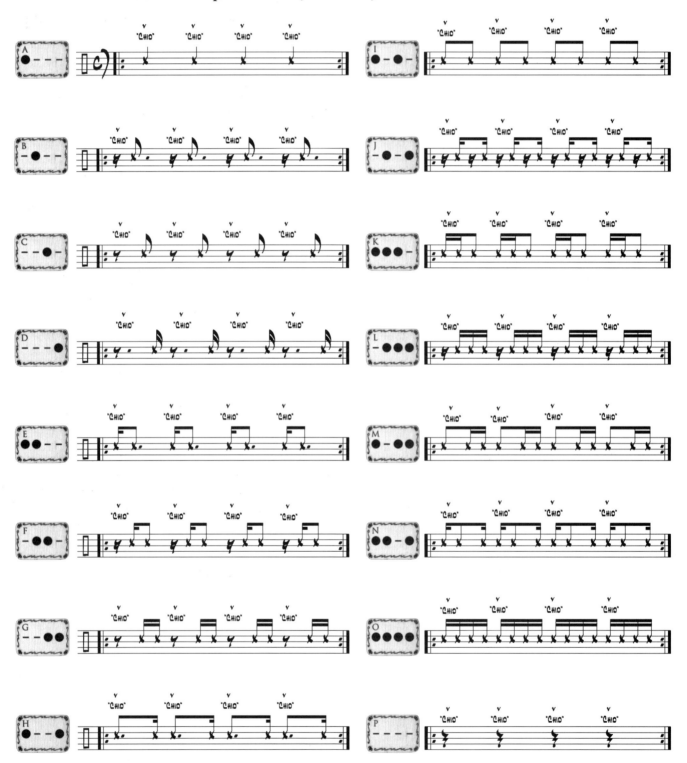

Warm-up Letters
BINARY A-P

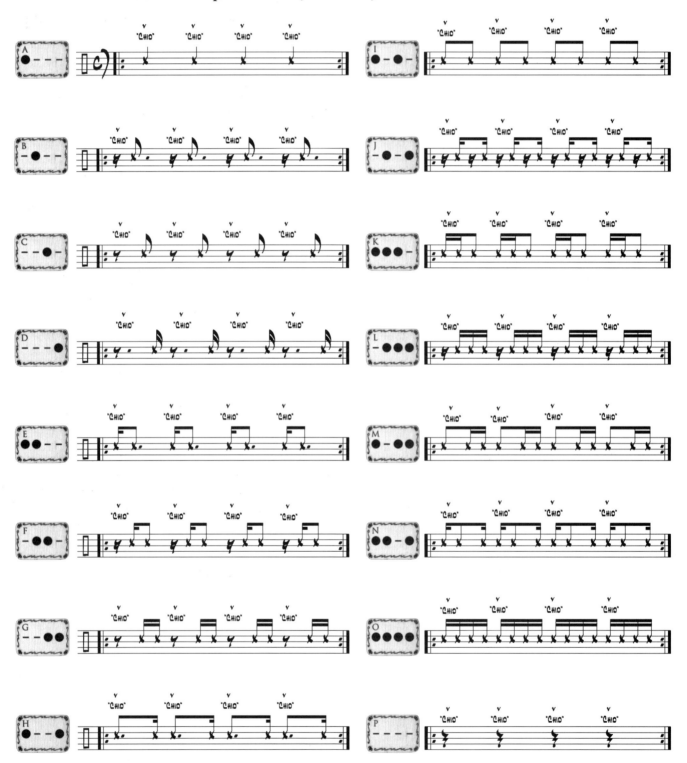

Let's begin with the binary letters, A-P.

Sing the tempo/quarter-note pulse with a short sound: "chid." The subdivision here is 16th notes, so one letter fits in one quarter note. The "instrumentation" is your hands clapping the dots. First practice the letters separately to get really comfortable with each one of them in relation to the quarter note (the "chid").

Now, the next step is to put the letters A-P together in an exercise. Play each bar four times before going on to the next one without stopping, while always singing the quarter note pulse (the "chid").

DATE:	TEMPOS:

For the ternary letters, the same principle applies, but the subdivision will be eighth-note triplets. Again, practice the letters separately at first.

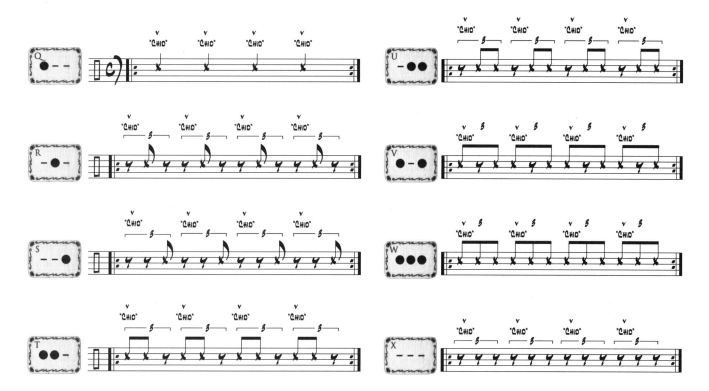

Now put the ternary letters into an exercise. Play each letter for four bars before going on to the next one without stopping, while always singing the quarter-note pulse (the "chid").

If you had a difficult time continuing the "chid" sound all the way through the exercises, you should check each of the letters separately before you try the whole exercise again. Vocalizing the "chid" sound is very important, because it will prevent you from shifting the downbeat or changing the tempo unintentionally while playing (this is a common mistake made by drummers, and often they don't even notice that it is happening!). If you are not completely solid with your timing and vocalizing, it will be difficult for you to execute the upcoming exercises in this book.

When you feel ready, let's pick up a pair of sticks and go to the next chapter.

CHAPTER 1: *Letters*

Part B - SNARE AND PAD EXERCISES

 Guide Track: 1-8

 Call and Response: 27-34

 Warm-up to Burnout: 43-48

Time Letters

SNARE AND PAD EXERCISES / BINARY A-P

 1,2

Now let's apply the Rhythmic Alphabet to the pad or snare drum.

Instead of clapping the letters like in the warm-up , simply go through the alphabet and play each letter with your sticks on the pad or snare drum.

Do this in three steps:

     1. First do it with your stronger hand.
     2. Then with your weaker hand, and finally...
     3. With both at the same time (try to avoid flamming).

DATE:	TEMPOS:
07.04.13	75
30.05.13	No 43 CD
31.05.13	No 43 CD
01.06.13	No 43 CD
04.06.13	No 43 CD

DATE:	TEMPOS:
49.5.13	60
21.5.13	60
24.5.13	55
31.05.13	No46 CD
01.06.13	No46 CD
01.06.13	No46 CD

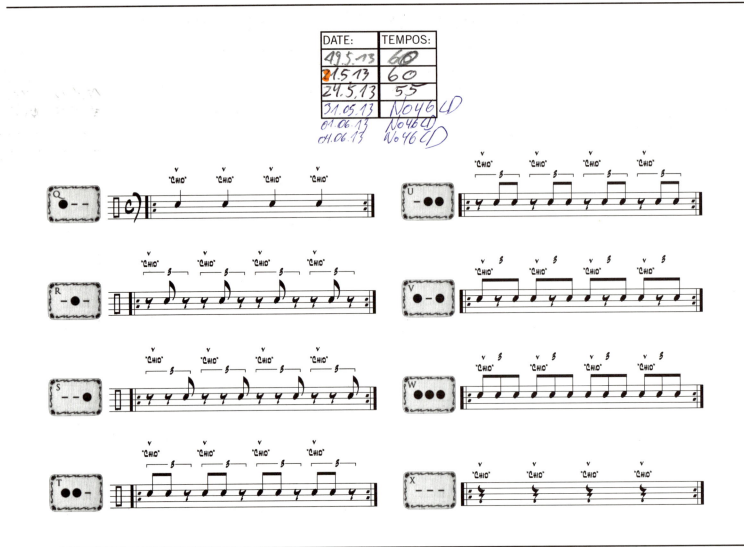

Dynamic Letters

SNARE AND PAD EXERCISES / BINARY A-P

This uses the alphabet as an accent/tap exercise by playing all notes of the subdivision. The notes that we clapped and played before are now accents in a flow of 16th notes. It's important to keep the unaccented notes low, which can be challenging, especially with the strokes right before or after an accent.

DATE:	TEMPOS:
04.09.13	50
05.04.13	60
07.05.13	55

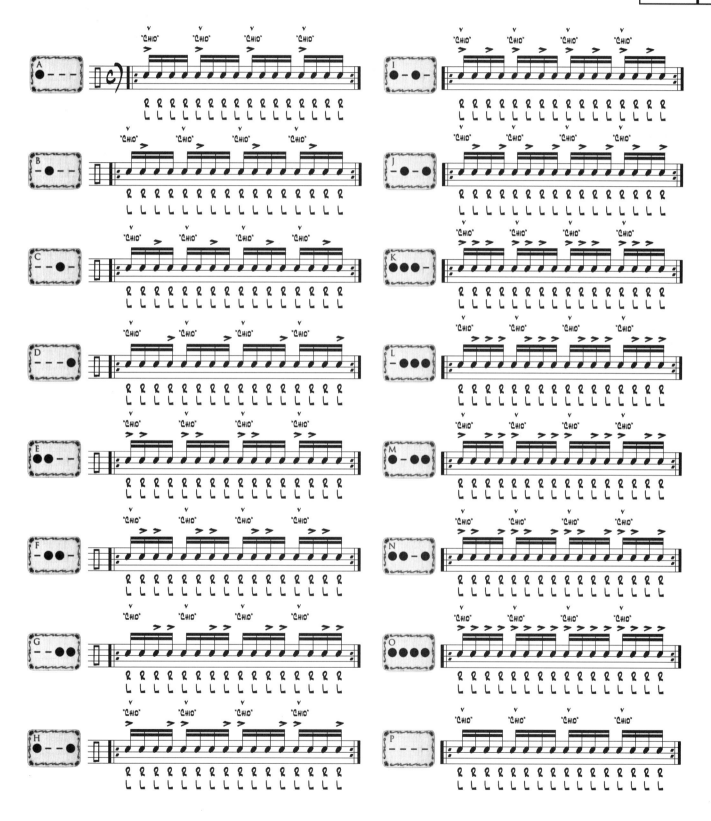

This page uses the alphabet as an accent/tap exercise within a flow of triplets. Remember to keep the unaccented notes low.

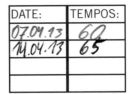

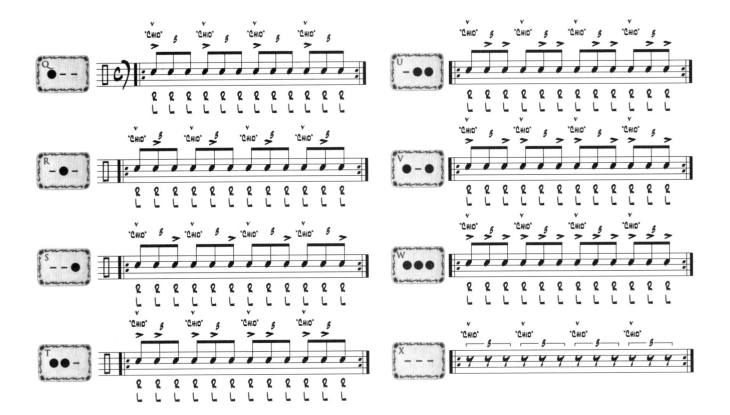

Sticking Letters
SNARE AND PAD EXERCISES / BINARY A-P

These patterns should sound the same as the dynamic letters but with different stickings:

1) **Hand-to-Hand Sticking:** The hands alternate from right to left.
2) **Right-Hand Lead:** Play the accents with the right hand and the unaccented notes with the left.
3) **Reverse Hand-to-Hand Sticking:** The hands alternate but start with the left.
4) **Left-Hand Lead:** Play the accents with the left hand and the unaccented notes with the right.

DATE:	TEMPOS:
1 23.04	50
2 8.09	50
3 5.5.13	50
4 9.5.13	50

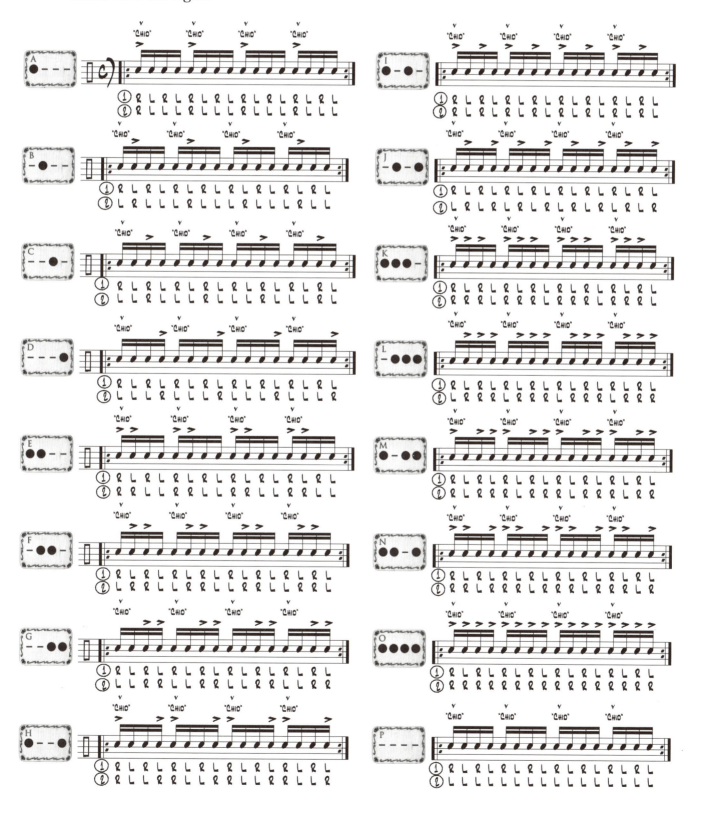

	DATE:	TEMPOS:
1	12.05.13	60
2	12.05.13	60

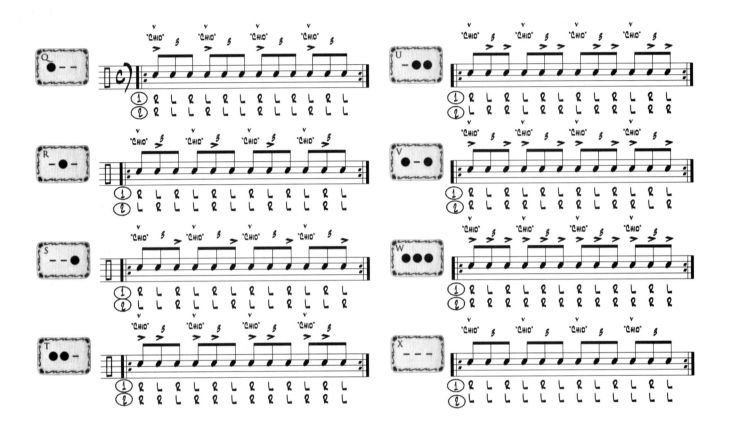

Now go through all previous sticking variations but without any dynamics/accents. This is a great way to get an even sound no matter what the sticking is. Stickings are a great tool to orchestrate ideas on the whole kit, so it is essential that your stickings aren't bound to a dynamic/accent pattern.

Now things get a little more interesting.

Diddles 1

Here we will add diddles on the right-hand accents, which means if we take the letter I, for example:

DATE:	TEMPOS:

this: *(musical notation)* **becomes:** *(musical notation)*

In this exercise, try not to accent the diddle at all. See it as a rhythmic variation with a constant dynamic.

DATE:	TEMPOS:

Here we apply diddles to the right-hand accents once again, this time with triplets.

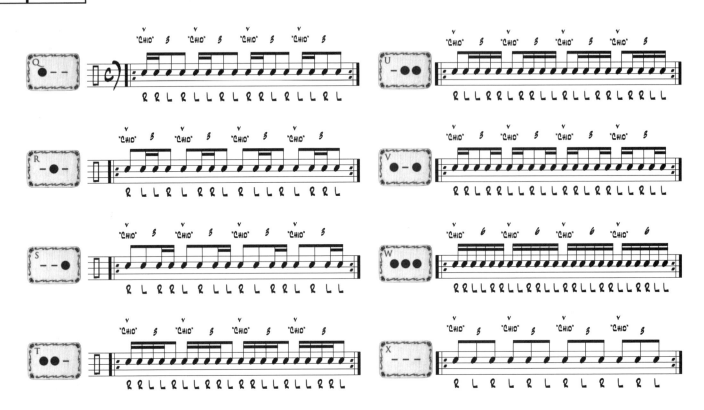

DATE:	TEMPOS:

Diddles 2. Now we will reverse the previous exercises: play the same accented letter patterns, but this time turn every unaccented note into a diddle.

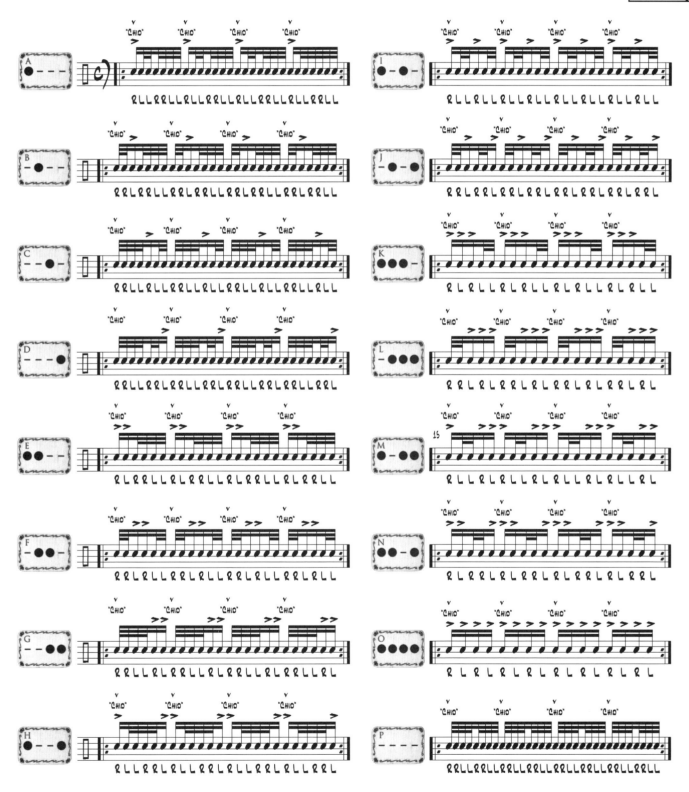

DATE:	TEMPOS:

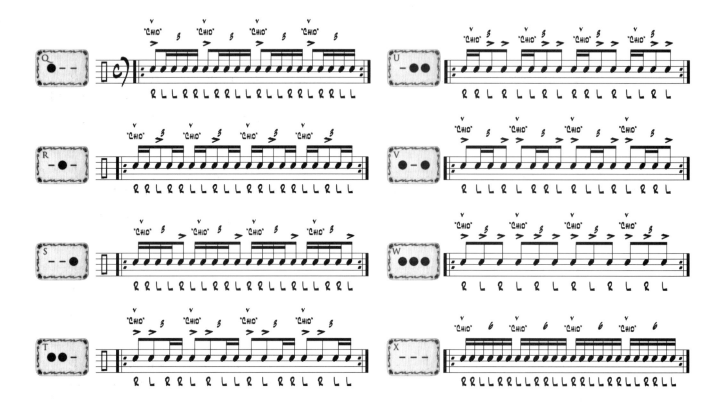

Rudimental Letters: Flams

SNARE AND PAD EXERCISES / BINARY A-P

Flams. Here, every accent becomes a flam. Take care that the original hand-to-hand sticking doesn't change at all. Just add the flam grace notes in the space before the principal hand stroke. So, if the accent is on the right hand, add the grace note with the left hand just before it. Reverse this for the left-hand flams.

DATE:	TEMPOS:

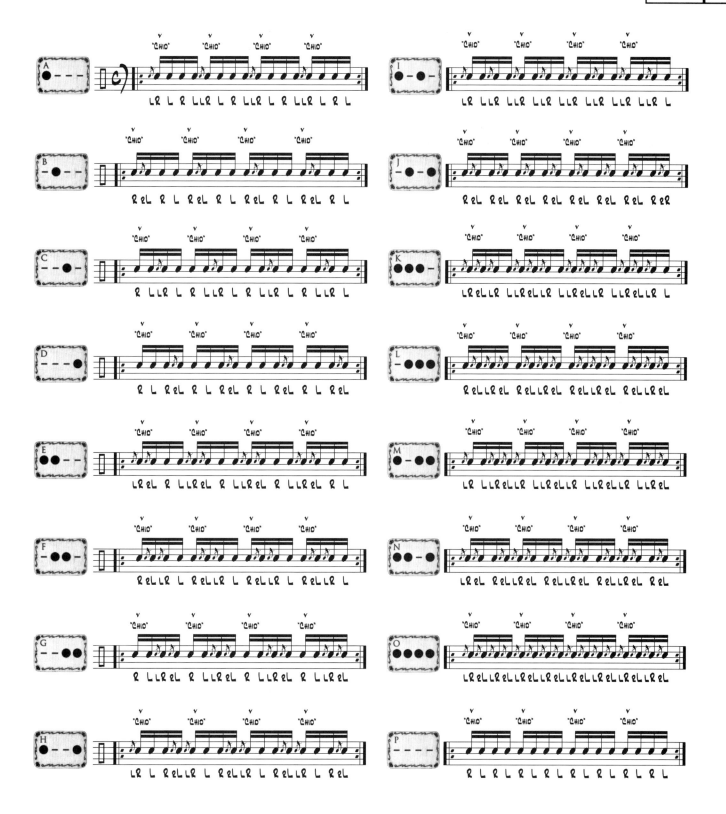

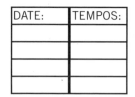

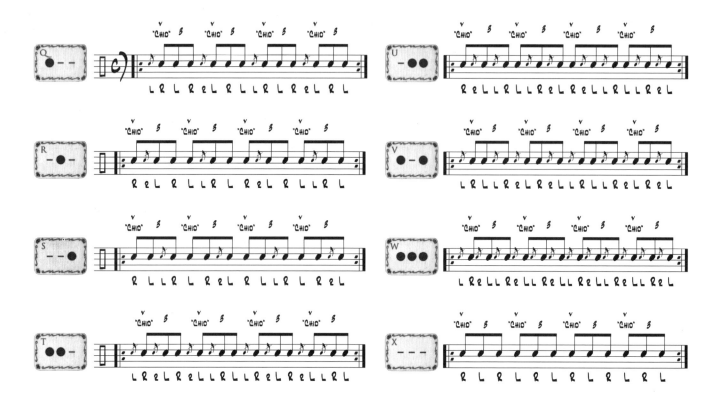

Rudimental Letters: Double-Note Singles

SNARE AND PAD EXERCISES / BINARY A-P

Double-Note Singles. Here's what I call Double-Note Singles. This is rhythmically the same thing that happens with the diddles on the accented notes (page 19), but the sticking is different. Now we use single strokes instead of diddles to create the same rhythm.

DATE: | TEMPOS:

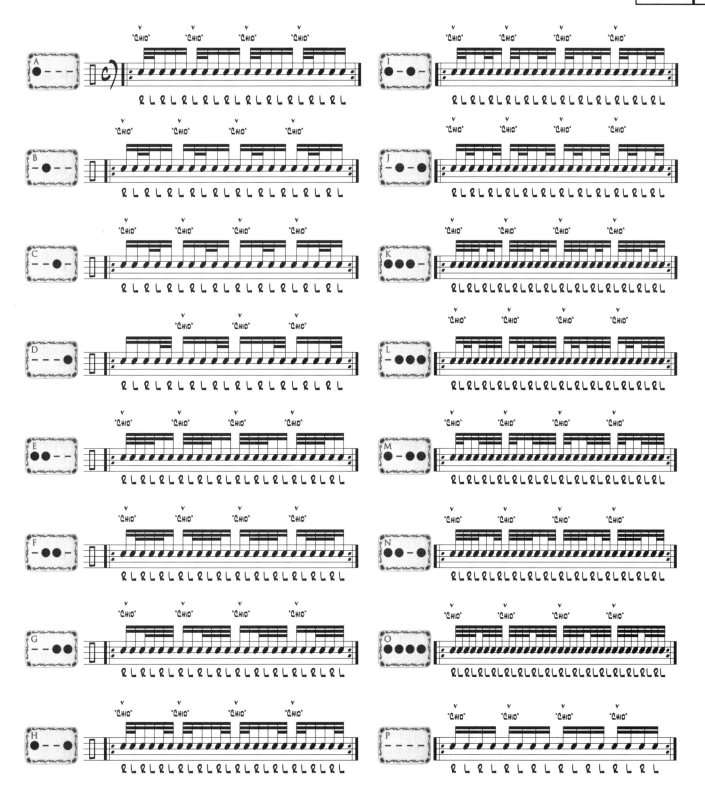

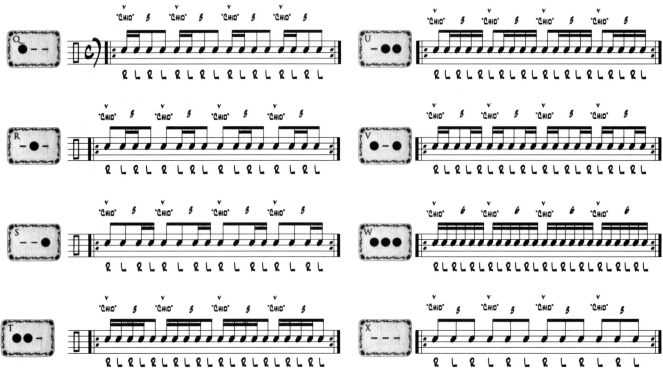

This vocabluary is extremely helpful when you want to get clean and fast doubles on deep and low-tuned toms. When you use single strokes, these rhythms speak much better than a diddle with one hand on low drums.

CHAPTER 1: *Letters*

Part C - DRUMSET LETTERS

Guide Track: 1-8

Call and Response: 27-34

Warm-up to Burnout: 43-48

Bass Drum Letters

BINARY A-P

DATE:	TEMPOS:
05.04.13	70
06.04.13	75
30.04.13	65
07.05.13	60

14.05.13 65
21.05.13 60
23.05.13 55
24.05.13 50
02.06.13 55
04.06.13 60

Let´s check out how these letters work in a groove setting.

Bass Drum Letters: Choose a simple ostinato for the other limbs like this one and play the alphabet with the bass drum.

Play the bass drum alphabet over the following ostinato:

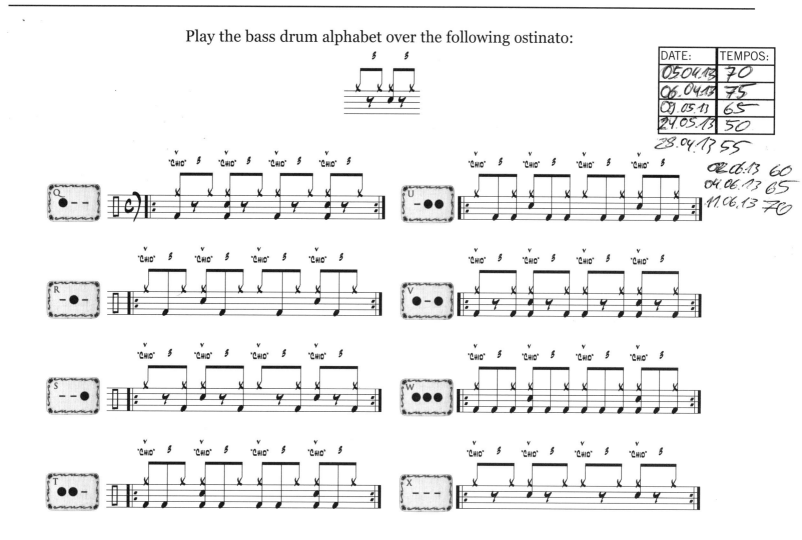

DATE:	TEMPOS:
05.04.13	70
06.04.13	75
09.05.13	65
24.05.13	50
28.04.13	55
02.06.13	60
04.06.13	65
11.06.13	70

Hi-Hat Letters 1

BINARY A-P

DATE:	TEMPOS:
07.04.13	75
23.04.13	70

Hi-Hat Letters 1: This will really strengthen your internal time feel because you can't rely on your right hand to play the subdivisions. Choose an ostinato to be played by the other limbs, for example: and play the alphabet with your right hand on the hi-hat.

Play the hi-hat alphabet over the following ostinato:

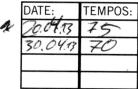

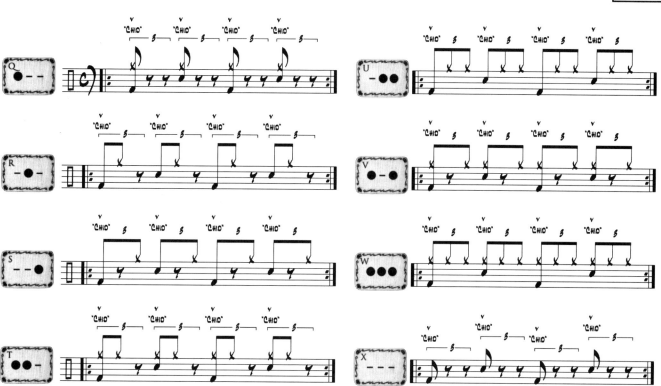

Hi-Hat Letters 2
BINARY A-P

DATE:	TEMPOS:
5.5.13	50
12.5.13	55

Hi-Hat Letters 2: This exercise should be relatively easy for your right-hand once you have mastered the dynamic workout, because it takes the exact rhythms from that workout and places them on the hi-hat with a simple ostinato on the bass drum and snare. Of course, it is a bit more challenging in terms of interdependence than the dynamic workout, because you have to add the other limbs to form a solid groove. These patterns are very useful in a musical situation. Make them feel good at different tempos, so when it comes to performing you don't have to worry about them.

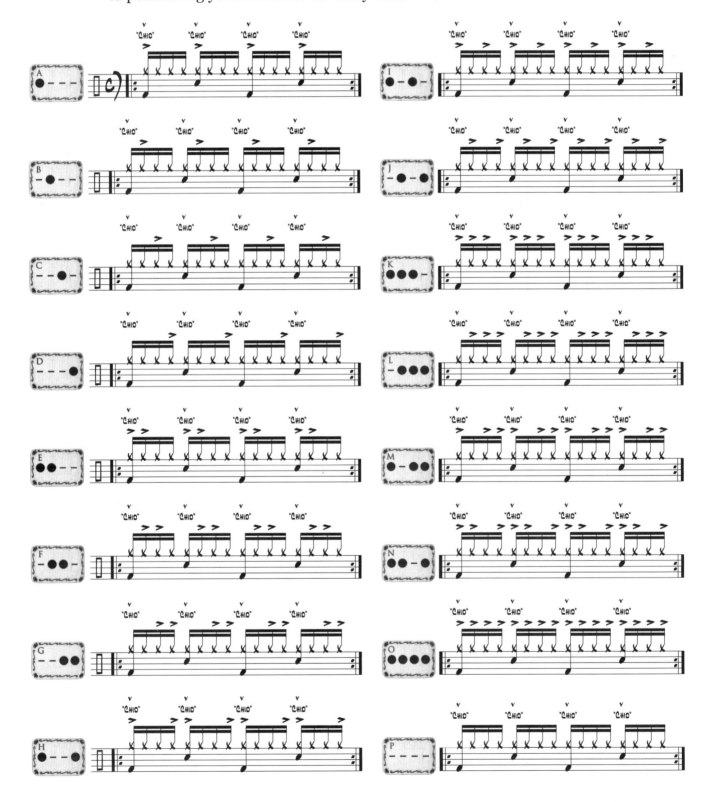

DATE:	TEMPOS:
12.5.13	60

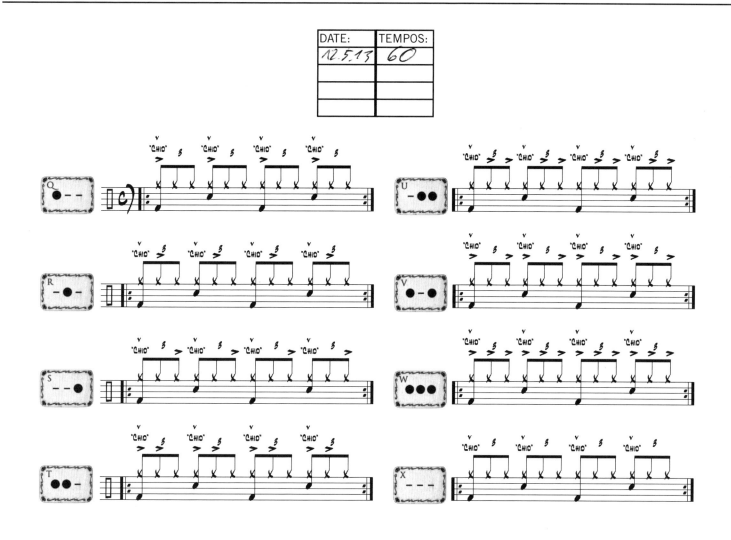

Also play on the ride cymbal instead of the hi-hat by playing the accent on the bell and the unaccented notes on the bow of the cymbal.

Hi-Hat Letters 3
BINARY A-P

Hi-Hat Letters 3: This is another great way to get different sounds out of your hi-hat. I always wondered why there aren´t any books out there that deal with this subject. So I came up with this variation. This is an exercise that will guide you through all possible ways of opening and closing the hi-hat in the subdivision you're in. At the same time it will also challenge your left-foot independence. This is a wonderful system to open up a whole other world of sound options on the hi-hat.

DATE:	TEMPOS:

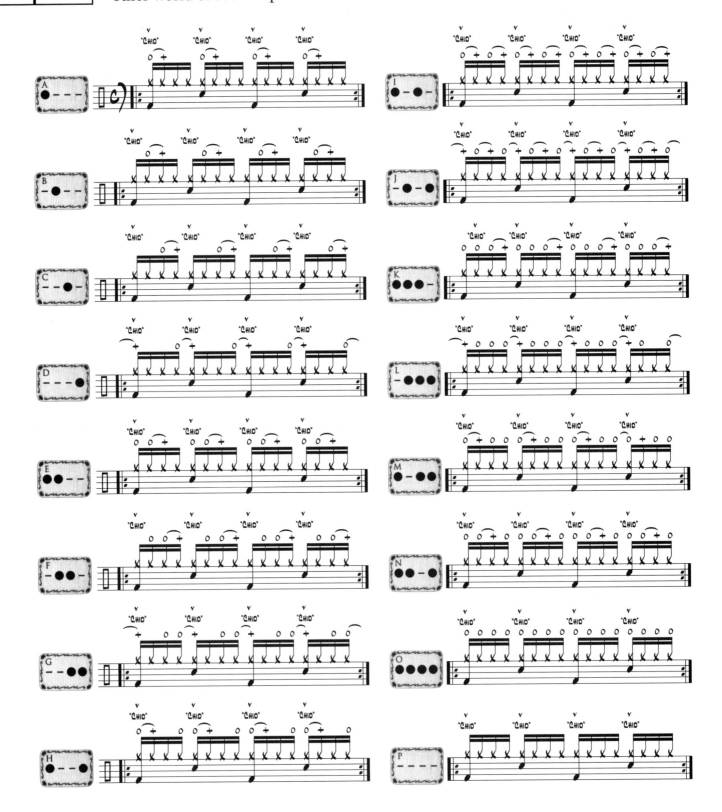

HI-HAT LETTERS 3 / TERNARY Q-X

DATE:	TEMPOS:

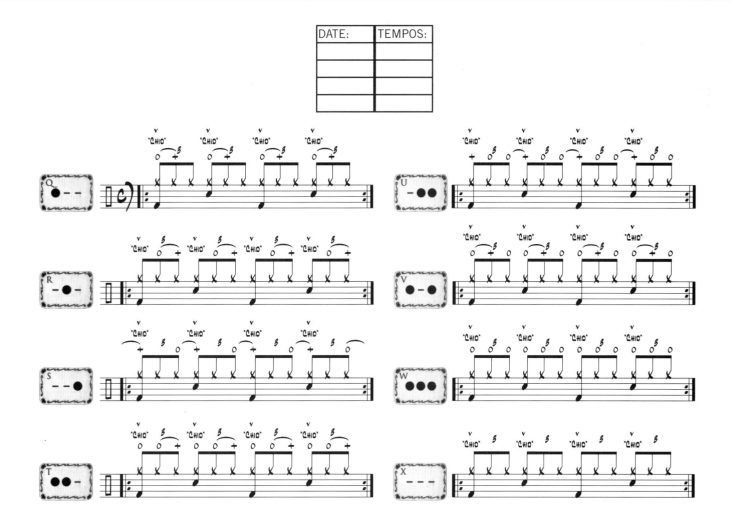

You can also play all of these exercises open-handed. For right-handed players, go back to page 30 and simply play the hi-hat with your left hand and snare drum with your right hand.

Then, if you have some time on your hands, also check out the next two pages!

Stepped Hi-Hat Letters

BINARY A-P

DATE:	TEMPOS:

WARNING!

This is very special and quite challenging. Some of the patterns you will come across in this exercise are a bit crazy—but some things sound very interesting. It will improve your independence and balance on the kit for sure, so check it out. Choose an ostinato to be played by the other limbs, for example: and play the alphabet with the left foot on the hi-hat.

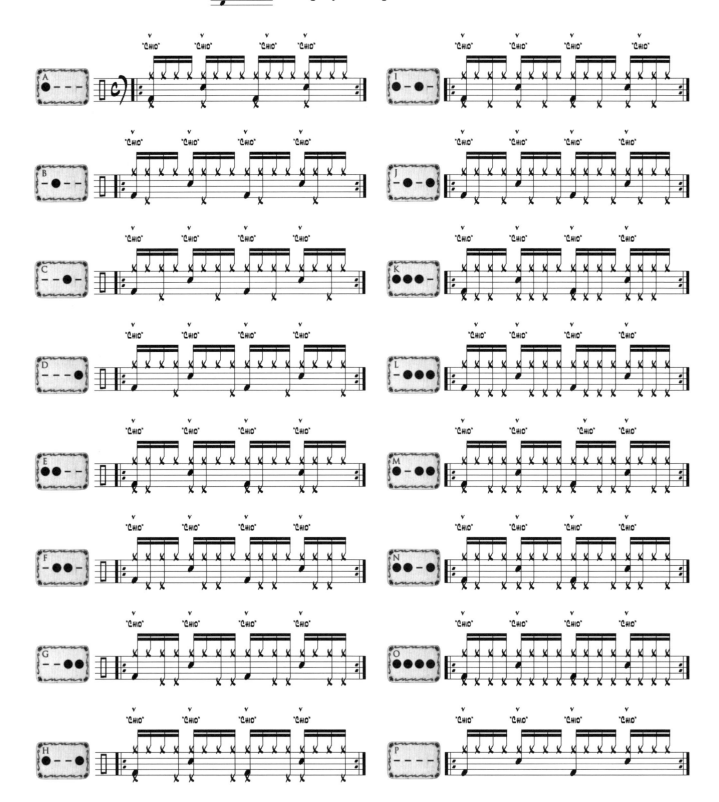

Choose an ostinato to be played by the other limbs, for example: 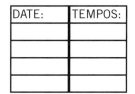 and play the alphabet with the left foot on the hi-hat.

DATE:	TEMPOS:

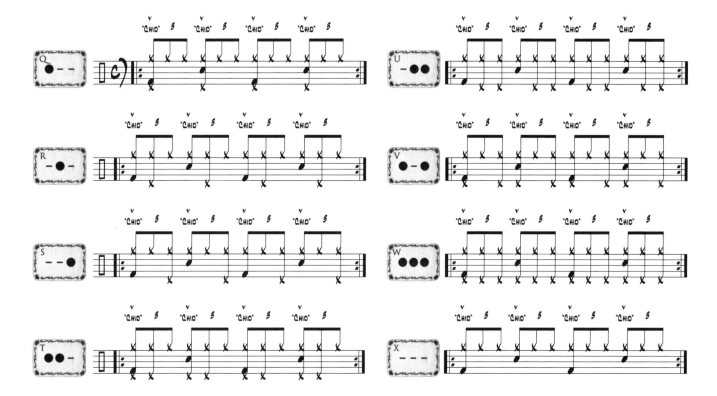

Ghosting Letters

BINARY A-P

DATE:	TEMPOS:

Ghosting Letters. Finally! I get asked about exercises for ghost notes all the time. Here is a system that should get you to a point where you don't have to worry about it anymore (at least technically). This deals with playing the alphabet as ghost notes on the snare while keeping a backbeat on 2 and 4.

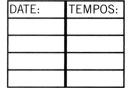

Next let's look at ghosting with the triplet alphabet—which will provide you with countless shuffle groove variations!

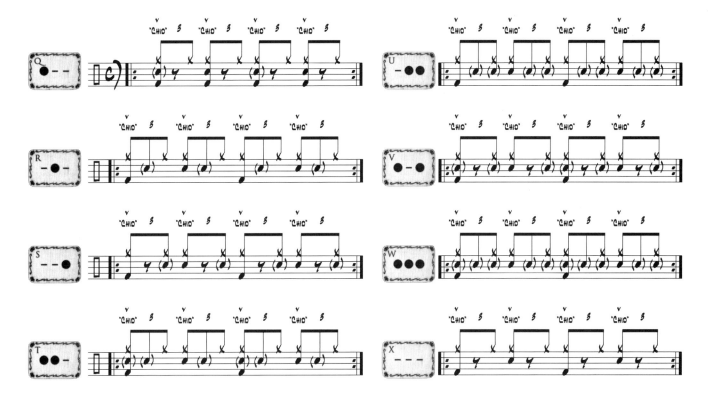

If you had problems getting these patterns up to speed, remember to play the ghost notes very low. This will help you to relax and get a good transparent sound when there is a big difference in the dynamic between ghost notes and backbeat.

GHOSTING LETTERS SWING / TERNARY Q-X

DATE:	TEMPOS:

Ghosting Letters: Swing Context. The DNA of a classic! A cool thing when using the triplet letters Q-X is when you apply it to the snare as left-hand ghost notes, while keeping a swing pattern on the ride cymbal and 2 & 4 on the hi-hat.

If you want to go further with this concept, go to pages 73 and 74 for more jazz independence.

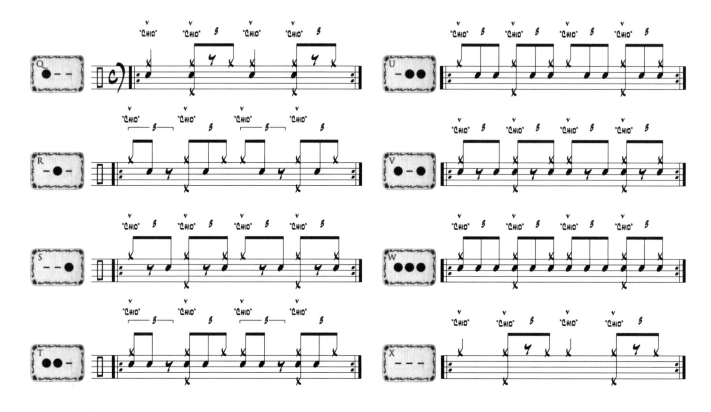

CHAPTER 2: *Words*

 **Call and Response: 9-12**

Words
ODD GROUPINGS

Time to take things to another level.

So far we've discussed the alphabet—16th & triplet quarter-note phrases—and although all longer phrases are made out of these elements, feeling and thinking in longer phases (one, two, or more bars) is an essential yet different skill. This is where we put meaningful words together into musical phrases.

The following systems have one goal: to help you to incorporate the letters into your repertoire by forming longer musical phrases, so you get comfortable using them in all kinds of combinations while seeing a bigger picture—and not thinking just in quarter-note phrases anymore.

This system of playing odd groupings over 16th or triplet subdivisions was first introduced to me by a former teacher of mine, Udo Dahmen. He totally changed my approach to drumming, and by practicing this system I gained a deeper understanding of music and rhythm.

Words: Introduction
THREES, FIVES, SEVENS / FIRST POSITION

Of course you can count these groupings like this:

Threes : 1 2 3 1 2 3 1 2 3 1 2 3 1 2 3 and 1

Fives: 1 2 3 4 5 1 2 3 4 5 1 2 3 4 5 and 1

But a more natural way of getting comfortable with phrases in three, five, and seven is by using phrases that you already use as words in everyday life that have three, five, or seven syllables, such as:

Threes: "ra-di-o"

Fives: "u-ni-ver-si-ty"

Sevens: "lis-ten to the ra-di-o"

So let's put them into a one-bar loop over a 16th-note subdivision, always starting them on the one.

Threes: radioradioradioradioradiora

Fives: universityuniversityuniversityu

Sevens: listentotheradiolistentotheradiolisten

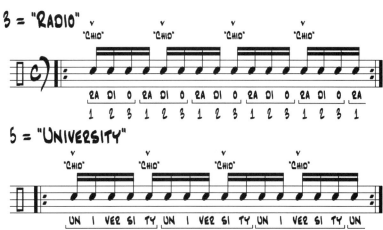

DATE:	TEMPOS:

Words

ACCENT PATTERNS / THREES, FIVES, SEVENS / FIRST POSITION

When we clap or play these groupings, we give them different accent patterns to identify them more clearly. Actually this is nothing that I have invented; this method of dividing fives and sevens into groups two and three has been done in classical Indian music for hundreds of years.

DATE:	TEMPOS:

3 is counted as 1 2 3.

5 is counted as 1 2 1 2 3.

7 is counted as 1 2 1 2 1 2 3.

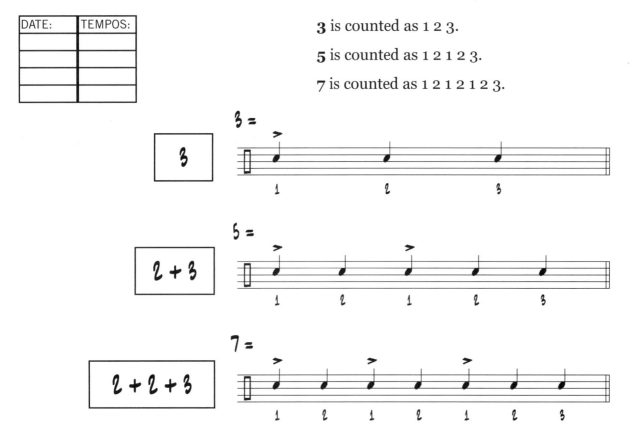

Now clap all the "1's" or just the accents from the accent patterns, and we will end up with this:

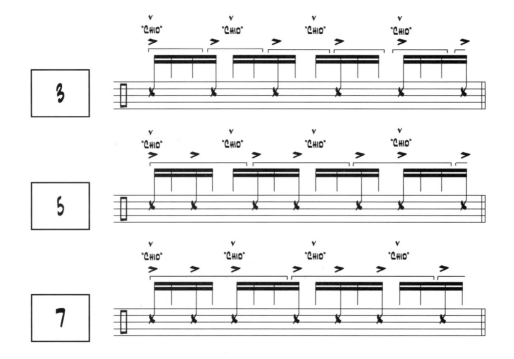

Rudimental Words
THREES / FIRST POSITION

Now we'll step into a new dimension by taking the word accent patterns and simply use them in the same way as we did with the alphabet. The cool thing is our hands don't have to do anything new. It now comes down to a mental challenge because the figures move over the quarter note. This will free you up to become more flexible with the alphabet vocabulary.

Let's take a closer look at the "radio" (the grouping of 3), and go through the rudiment applications that are available.

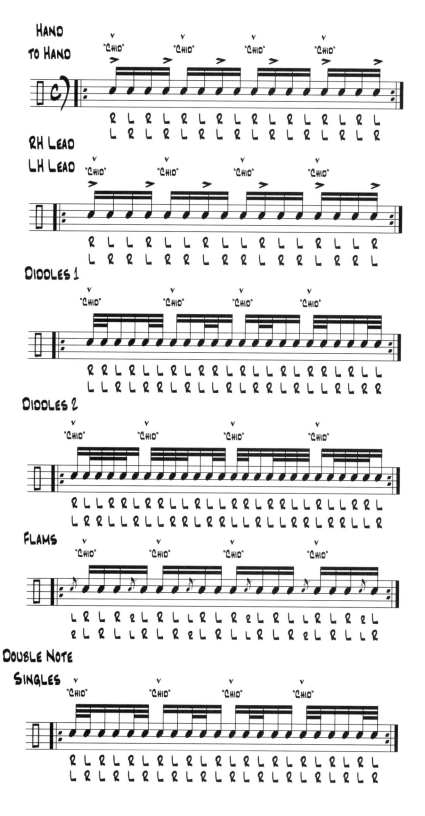

DATE:	TEMPOS:

Drumset Words
THREES / FIRST POSITION

This is the "radio" grouping of three applied as bass drum, right hand, and left-hand parts.

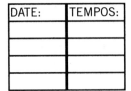

Here the backbeat and ghosting pattern fall on the same beat. When you play the ghostings on the snare, play an accent/backbeat here. When you play the ghostings as a pattern with your left hand on another drum, play the backbeat with your right hand on the snare at the same time.

Rudimental Words

FIVES / FIRST POSITION

Here are the rudiment applications of the grouping of five ("university").

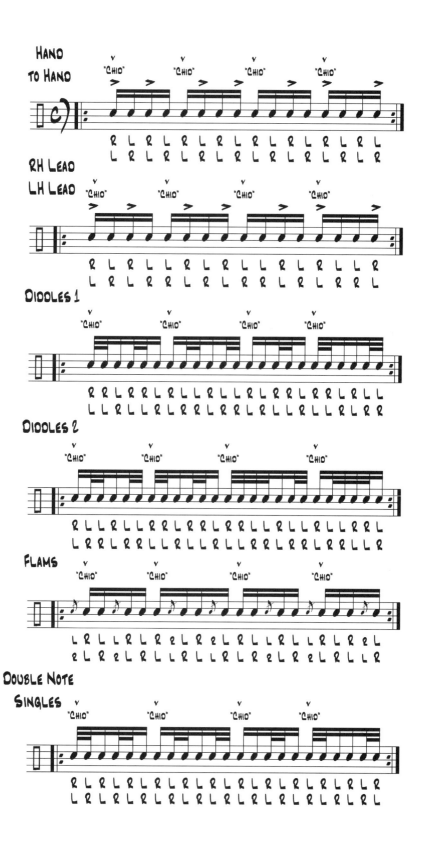

Drumset Words

FIVES / FIRST POSITION

This is the "university" grouping of five applied as bass drum, right hand, and left-hand drumset parts.

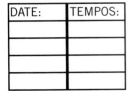

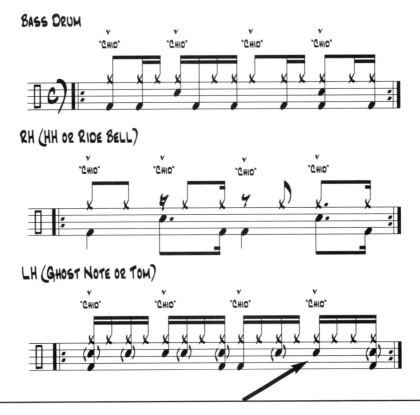

Here the backbeat and ghosting pattern fall on the same beat. When you play the ghostings on the snare, play an accent/backbeat here. When you play the ghostings as a pattern with your left hand on another drum, play the backbeat with your right hand on the snare at the same time.

Rudimental Words

SEVENS / FIRST POSITION

Here are the rudiment applications of the grouping of seven ("listen to the radio").

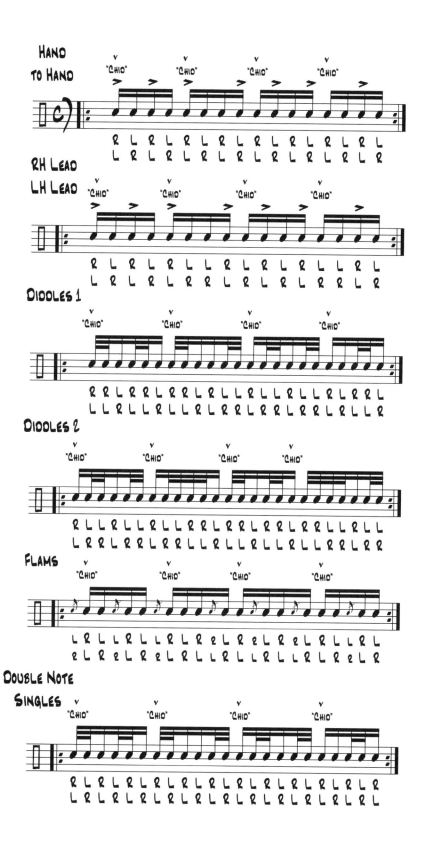

Drumset Words
SEVENS / FIRST POSITION

Finally, we have the "listen to the radio" grouping of seven applied as bass drum, right hand, and left-hand drumset parts.

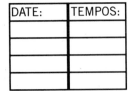

Here the backbeat and ghosting pattern fall on the same beat. When you play the ghostings on the snare, play an accent/backbeat here. When you play the ghostings as a pattern with your left hand on another drum, play the backbeat with your right hand on the snare at the same time.

Rudimental Words
THREES / SECOND POSITION

Positions: In all the exercises so far, the words always began on the one. Now, to get more flexibility and expanded vocabulary, we can start them in different positions: one or two 16th notes later. In the previous exercises the groupings were called the "first position." As we move to these rhythms that start on the second or third 16th note, we call it—right!—the second or third position.

Drumset Words

THREES / SECOND POSITION

DATE:	TEMPOS:

Rudimental Words

FIVES / SECOND POSITION

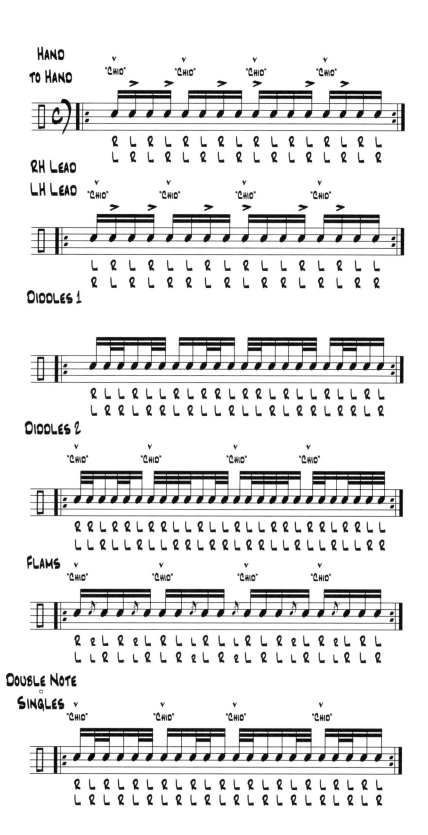

Drumset Words

FIVES / SECOND POSITION

DATE:	TEMPOS:

Rudimental Words
SEVENS / SECOND POSITION

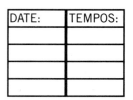

Drumset Words
SEVENS / SECOND POSITION

DATE: | TEMPOS:

DATE:	TEMPOS:

Here the backbeat and ghosting pattern fall on the same beat. When you play the ghostings on the snare, play an accent/backbeat here. When you play the ghostings as a pattern with your left hand on another drum, play the backbeat with your right hand on the snare at the same time.

Rudimental Words

THREES / THIRD POSITION

With the "radio" grouping of three, it also makes sense to do a third position, so here it is.

DATE:	TEMPOS:

Drumset Words
THREES / THIRD POSITION

DATE:	TEMPOS:

Hi-Hat Words
THREE, FIVE, and SEVEN

This is a hi-hat accent version of all the previous groupings. It's very useful vocabluary that adds some spice even in straighter or slower grooves.

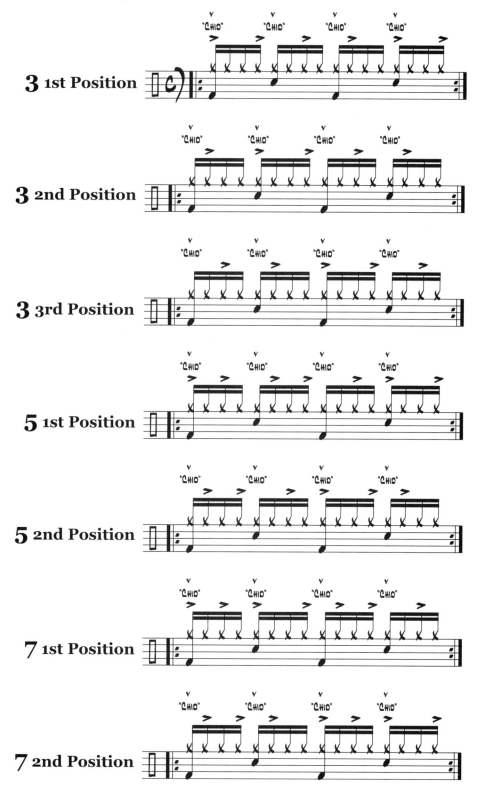

DATE:	TEMPOS:

Also practice these examples on the ride cymbal by playing the accents on the bell ✗ and the unaccented notes on the bow of the cymbal. ➤

Hi-Hat Words

FIVE and SEVEN / TERNARY

Now let's check out some ternary hi-hat examples.

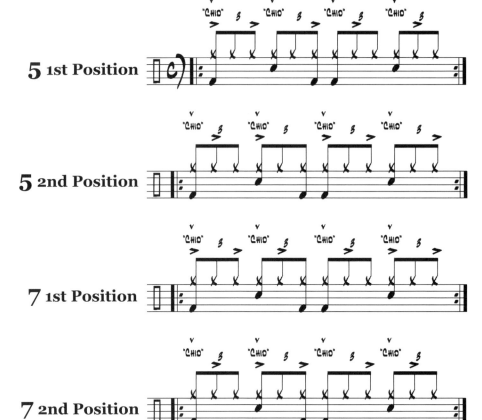

5 1st Position

5 2nd Position

7 1st Position

7 2nd Position

Also practice these examples on the ride cymbal by playing the accents on the bell and the unaccented notes on the bow of the cymbal.

Words Recap Sheets

Let's put all that we've learned together into a more practical context. So far we played the words starting in different positions. Now let's breathe more life into them by mixing them together. You'll find numbers like 31 or 52 between the barlines. The big number represents the grouping to play, while the smaller number represents the position it should appear in.

I couldn't possibly write out all the different ways that you can play this, but here are some exercises to start with:

1. Play as grooves utilizing the three variations from this chapter (BD,LH,RH: each limb plays the specified rhythm while the other limbs keep time).

2. Play as a snare drum etude by utilizing the rudiments and stickings of this chapter

3. Play as grooves, but make every fourth bar as a fill by applying the rudiments and stickings ideas.

4. Play in ternary subdivision.

This is also a great thing to do together with your bass player. If your bass player learns the rhythms in this book, you can read/play these patterns together as a rhythm section, and make use of the jam tracks on the CD.

WORDS RECAP SHEET 1

DATE:	TEMPOS:

15,16,22,23

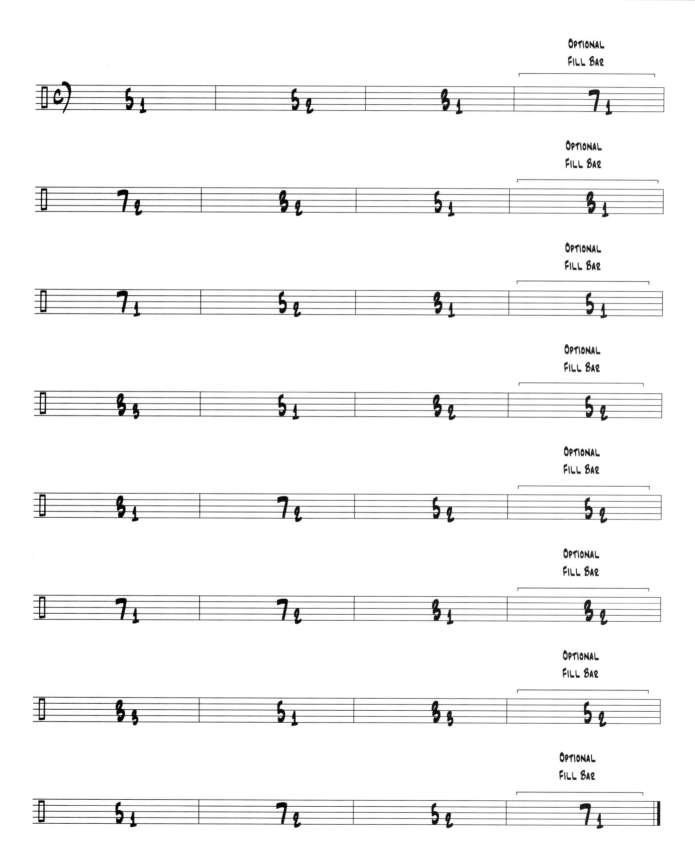

17,18,24,25,26

DATE: | TEMPOS:

Independence Words

We can also use the words to create some interesting independence or interdependence ideas. One simple way of doing that is just to divide the words up between the feet and the hands. First, practice each ostinato separately, and when you comfortable, add the second layer.

Combine all of the foot patterns with the hand patterns and find different orchestrations for them. There is a lot you can get out of these. Have fun.

DATE:	TEMPOS:

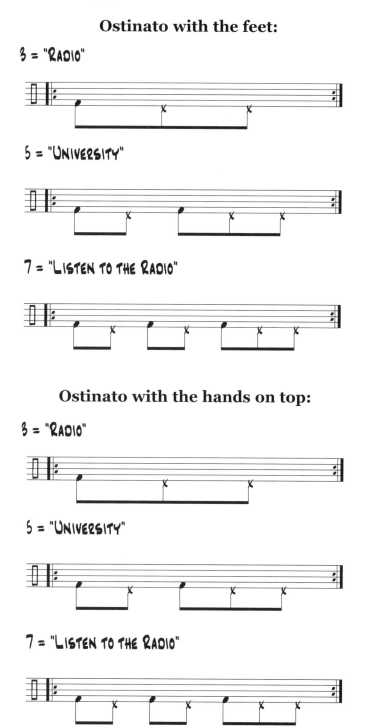

Ostinato with the feet:

3 = "Radio"

5 = "University"

7 = "Listen to the Radio"

Ostinato with the hands on top:

3 = "Radio"

5 = "University"

7 = "Listen to the Radio"

Note: Practice playing the foot patterns while improvising on top with the hands.

If you've mastered this, great. But please then make up your own combinations and create longer phrases. Explore what else is possible. You now know the building blocks; use them!

CHAPTER 3: *Syntax*

Syntax

Binary / Form: Two-Bar Phrases
Subdivision = ♫

Let's take it one step further with rhythmic syntax. OK, here's how it works:

Choose a subdivision and how long the phrase should be, then randomly write down the numbers 3, 5, and 7 as long as they fit inside your phrase. If they don't, simply add the number that you need at the end to make the bar complete. For example, let's say your subdivision is sixteenth notes, and the phrase should be two bars. That means you'd have 32 sixteenth notes that you can divide however you want.

For example:

3 5 7 3 5 7 (+2)

5 5 7 7 3 3 (+2)

7 7 7 3 5 3

3 5 7 7 3 7

7 5 7 3 3 7

3 5 3 5 7 3 3 3

5 3 7 3 5 7 (+2)

DATE:	TEMPOS:

Syntax

With two bars of triplet subdivision, you can play phrases like this:

Ternary / Form: Two-Bar Phrases
Subdivision = ♪♪♪

DATE:	TEMPOS:

3 3 3 3 3 3 3 3

5 5 5 7 (+2)

7 3 7 3 3 (+1)

5 3 5 3 5 3

7 3 7 5 (+2)

7 5 7 3 (+2)

5 7 5 5 (+2)

7 5 7 5

Syntax
APPLICATION EXAMPLES

Now, with syntax, you have a more advanced blueprint that you can use with all the applications that we have already checked out. Here are some examples of how you can use this powerful system.

3 5 7 3 5 7 (+2)

DATE:	TEMPOS:

Sticking Variations

Rudimental Variations

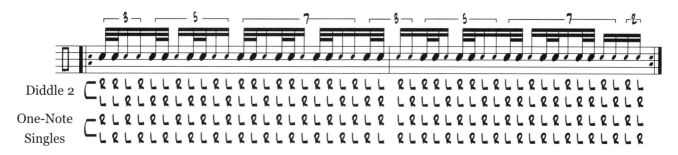

Groove Application   Ostinato

Groove Application 2   Ostinato

CHAPTER 4: *Advanced Language*

Advanced Language

With the following concepts and ideas I really want to get you thinking about the sheer endless possibilities of what can be done with this system. This chapter is bigger than it looks because written out it would have been at least two or three other books! Instead, the next pages will contain suggestions of how to combine some of the previous exercises in this book to create even more new variations.

I assume that you have worked through the previous champters and know them inside out. So we will move a bit faster here. I want to leave you with as many concepts as possible that can be applied to all of the previous chapters

Linear Language 1
Linear Letters: Binary

You can basically think of the linear language as an application of the sticking letters principle (pages 17 and 18). But now, divide the letters not only between right and left hand, but also between the hands and feet.

Here is one possible example with the letter E:

RH: stays as the right-hand part, played on the floor tom.
LH: becomes the bass drum part with the right foot.

Notation 1

A cool way to get comfortable with this is to apply a backbeat to it, while the left foot plays 8th notes on the hi-hat.

Ostinato

Linear Language 1
BINARY

Here is what it would look like with letters I through N.

DATE:	TEMPOS:

Linear Language 1
TERNARY

In the ternary world we can apply the same concept. Here we can take the notes from the right hand, and play them with the left foot/hi-hat.

Notation 1

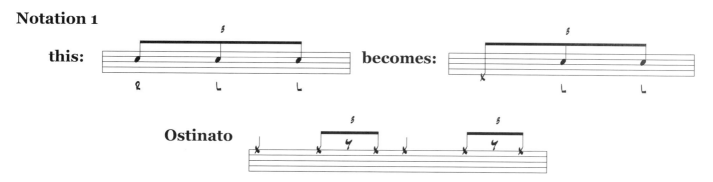

In this exercise the right hand will play the swing ride cymbal pattern. By approaching the patterns this way, hopefully you will find this to be more than just a challenging jazz independence workout. It should help you to create new vocabulary. When you listen closely to what contemporary jazz drummers play, you will be surprised how much you will recognize from the following exercises in their repertoire. This exercise will enable you to get comfortable with these combinations yourself, so you can add them to your bag of tricks.

DATE:	TEMPOS:

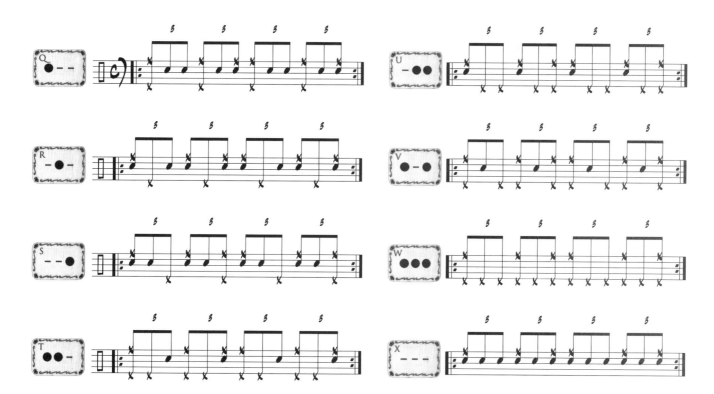

Also practice with the bass drum in place of the hi-hat, and add a 2 & 4 on the left foot/hi-hat.

Linear Language 1
TERNARY

Linear Words: Let's move on and apply the same linear principle to the RH lead of the words. Let's stay in the jazz context and take a look how the fives and sevens work with this idea. Now it gets really interesting!

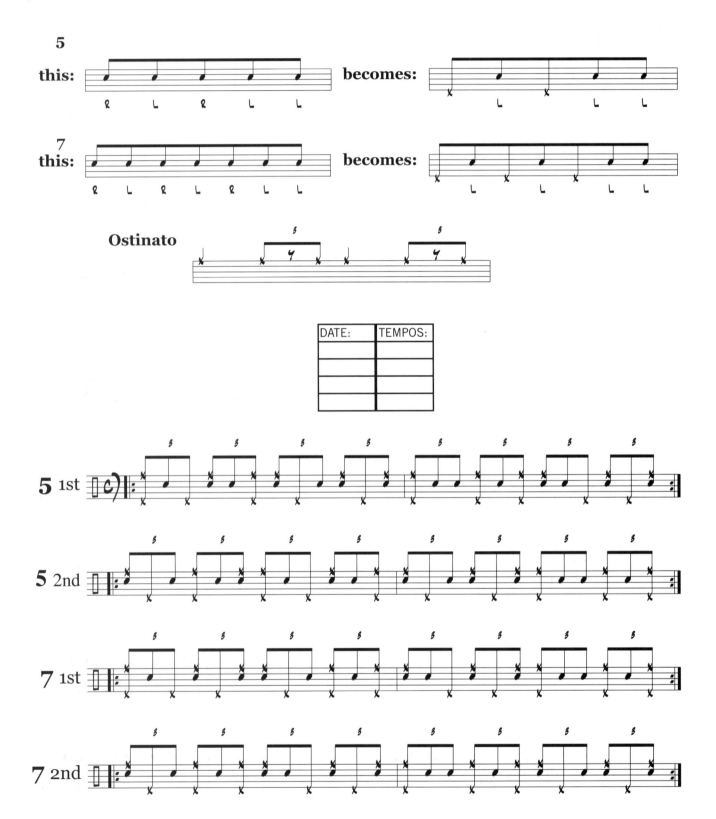

Linear Language 1
BINARY

When we think about the words in binary subdivision, my suggestion would be to approach this in three ways. Here's the first approach:

1A: Play steady quarter- or eighth-note offbeat time with your left-foot hi-hat, and play the R's with the bass drum and the L's with both hands together. Play each hand on a different surface; for example, play the left hand on snare and the right hand on a floor tom. This is great because you train both hands at the same time. This stuff reminds me of the kind of licks Tony Williams used.

1B: Reverse of 1A: Do it the other way around. This time the bass drum will play the L's and the hands will play the R's.

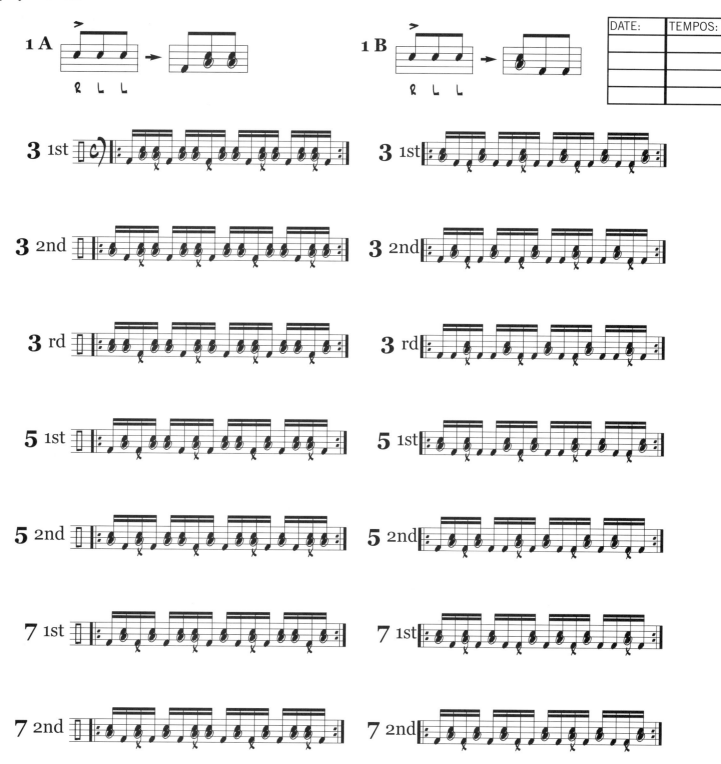

Linear Language 2
BINARY

Here's the second approach to applying the binary linear words on the drumset:

2A: Play the R's with the right foot on the bass drum and ride cymbal together, while the L's are played by the left hand on the snare drum.

2B: Reverse of 2A: The R's are now played by the left hand on the snare, and the L's by right foot on bass drum and right hand on the ride.

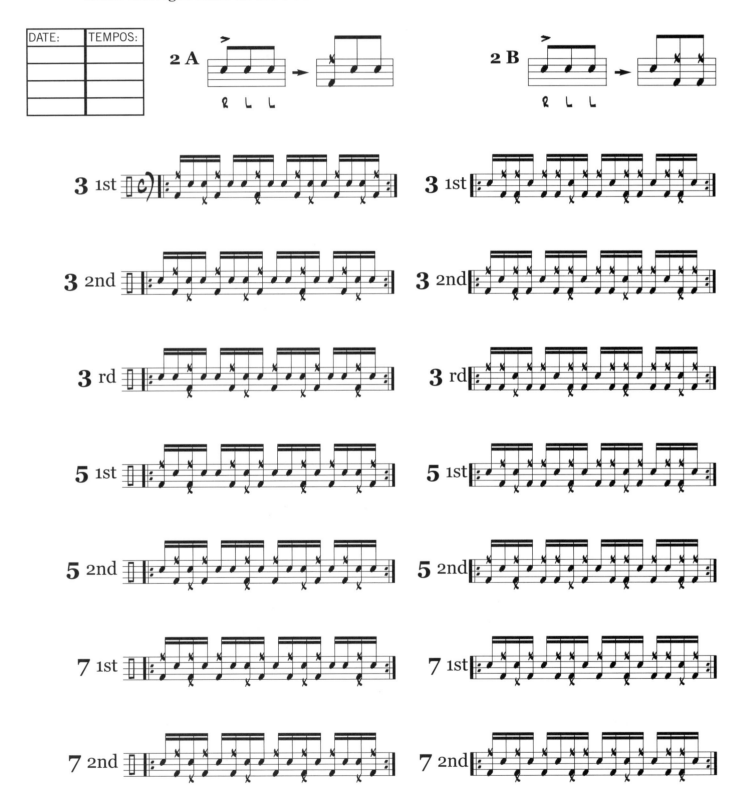

Linear Language 2
BINARY

I don't like the idea of "licks," but if you are hungry for some, here they are.

This is an orchestration idea for the linear words that sounds really interesting: Play the note that comes after the accent on a tom instead of on the snare. That would look something like this: *(Don't forget that it's always good to keep eighth or quarter notes with the left foot going through stuff like this.)*

DATE:	TEMPOS:

1. Also apply this concept also to the second positions of the words, and move the tom notes onto different toms.
2. Also apply the same concepts/routines to the ternary subdivision words.
3. Finally, mix them together by using the Words Recap Sheets 1, 2, and 3 (pages 62-64).

Linear Language 3

BINARY

DATE:	TEMPOS:

Here's the third approach to applying the binary linear words on the drumset. Now we'll free up the right hand to play time in eighth notes, while the R's and L's are divided up between LH and RF.

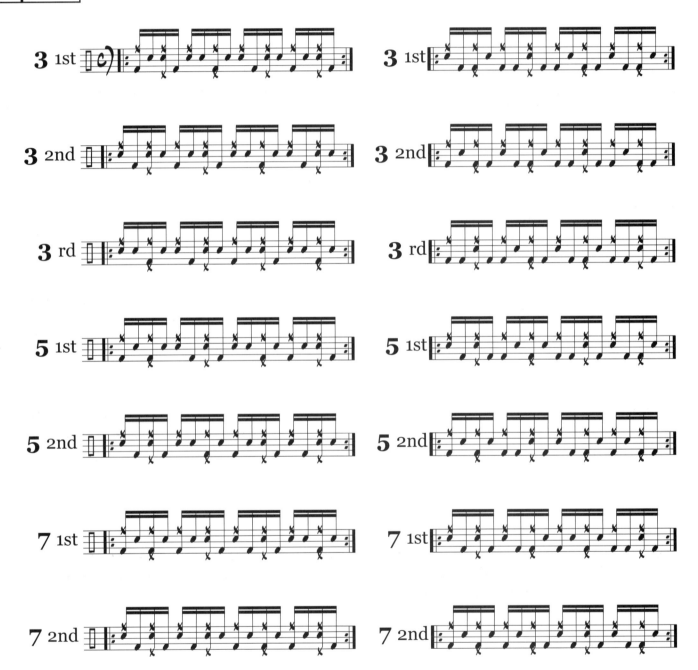

When you are comfortable with this, trying playing different ostinatos with the right hand. Need some ideas? See the following page!

Quick List
HI-HAT / RIDE CYMBAL PATTERNS

Here I've put together the "Top 7" most popular hi-hat & ride cymbal patterns that you find in contemporary music. This chart is useful in creating practical variations for drumset exercises right away. Simply replace the right-hand pattern that's written with one of the following cymbal patterns.

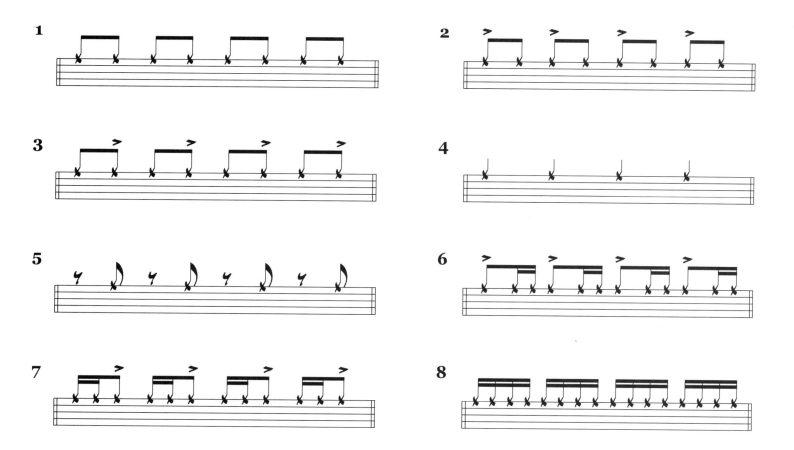

Of course if you want a comprehensive, all-embracing pratice approach, you can simply take the letters of the rhythmic alphabet and make them into your hi-hat or ride cymbal variations! Take it as far as you want!

Accent Language
SPEAKING WITH AN ACCENT

Accents are a simple but very effective way to elevate all your vocabulary to another level. Dynamics really change the way we experience phrases. You'll feel this when you play the following exercises.

Sometimes, when adding accents, it can even be difficult to keep the original phrase as a guideline in your head, because your ears are telling you that you're playing something completely different. And they're right! Accents will make a given pattern sound completely different. You will find that exploring the world of accents is a fantastic source for new material. Let's go!

One way of approaching the application of accents, is to superimpose accents in the patterns of the rhythmic alphabet as a new layer over another exercise. For example, let's use the letters A through D as a blueprint for placing the accents, and use letter A of the sticking workout (pages 17 and 18) as the basic pattern for it. Here's what this would look like:

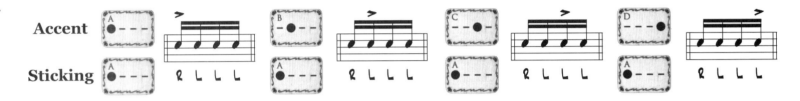

Remember, you can do this with every letter of the sticking workout (or really any binary exercise), and with the entire rhythmic alphabet superimposed as accents over it.

And if you want to go ternary, then use the ternary letters, of course!

A more advanced exercise would involve taking a rudimental phrase (in this example I've used one from the flam rudiments, pages 23 and 24) and move the accent through every note of the pattern.

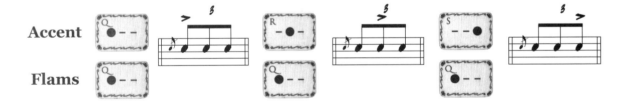

Again, remember that you can apply the same concept with the entire alphabet has accent variations.

Or how about this one? What if we take the accent pattern, and make it a fixed point, and then move the rudiment around. This should be the same in theory, but it feels quite different when you play them after each other. Check this out, and remember that, again, I have presented just the first three combinations. Take this as far as you want!

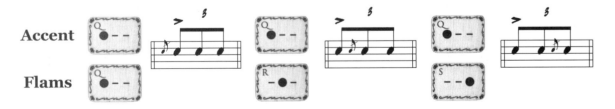

SPEAKING WITH AN ACCENT

Here is one last thing on the rudiments with accents:

Let's move one accent through a pattern that has more than 4 notes. Try the double-note singles, for example:

DATE:	TEMPOS:

Single Accents: Notation 1   **Double Accents:** Notation 2

This, by the way, is one of my favorite warm-up exercises, because the sticking turns around after each phrase. Have fun with it!

Remember, these written out examples are just dealing with the double-note singles pattern of the letter A. You can:

1. Apply the same concept to the whole alphabet of the double-note singles (pages 25 and 26).

2. Then, go through all the other rudiment applications and move the accent through those patterns. This will add a completely new level to the exercises on pages 19-26.

SPEAKING WITH AN ACCENT

On the drumset you could do things like this:

Take one instrument (like the snare drum) within a linear approach and put accents in different places. To demonstrate, let's use one example from the linear language to create more variations by just using different accents on the snare drum.

As with many of the previous examples, you can use this principle with many of the previous exercises.

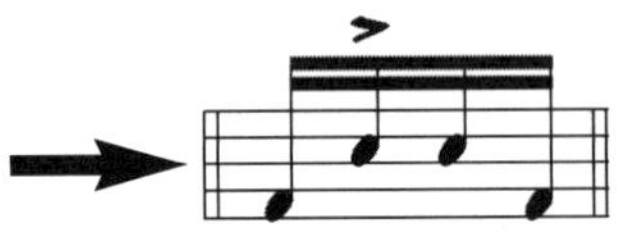

Combination Ex. 1

Combination Ex. 2

Combination Ex. 3

Combined Rudiments
LETTERS

When it comes to rudiments, the next level is to combine different rudiments into one phrase. This concept is very simple, but the execution of the material can be quite challenging. Again, we will be using simple building blocks from the letters, and using them to create some Frankenstein monsters of the rudiment world!

Here is a simple formula that will allow you to build countless numbers of hybrid rudiments:

Take the rudiment letters and combine all A-Ps with all A-Ps and all Q-Xs with all Q-Xs. For example, here I chose the flam letter Q, and want to apply it to the other ternary letters (Q-X). It would look like this:

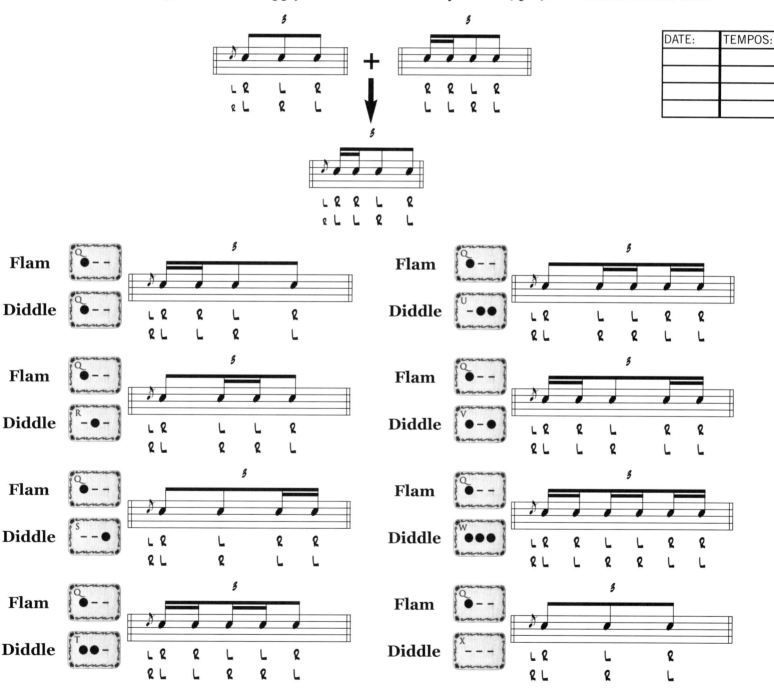

Now you can do the same thing with the letter R from the flam letters with Q-X from the Diddles 2, and then flam letter S, and so on. Eventually go through all the letters by using this system. I myself try to do a new one every day—there are a lot!

Syntax Revisited
A NEW WORD? FOUR-NOTE GROUPINGS

Well, actually this word isn't new because we've covered all four-note phrases already with the letters A-P. In our previous syntax examples (pages 67-68), we use groupings of three, five, and seven. But it adds a little more fun and variety to put in a word in for four as well.

If you want to get comfortable by clapping and speaking the words, simply use "e-le-va-tor" for four, and combine it with the other words in the syntax chapter.

Here are some syntax examples with fours. Have fun with them!

DATE:	TEMPOS:

Binary / Form: Two-Bar Phrases
Subdivision = ♫♫

3 4 5 7 5 7 (+1)

5 4 7 4 7 5

5 4 7 7 3 5 (+1)

7 5 7 4 5 4

4 5 4 7 5 7

7 5 4 7 5 4

5 4 4 7 5 4 3

7 7 4 5 4 5

Syntax Revisited

A NEW WORD? FOUR-NOTE GROUPINGS

With the triplets/ternary examples, the grouping of four is especially interesting because it also moves the downbeat.

DATE:	TEMPOS:

Ternary / Form: Two-Bar Phrases

Subdivision = ♪♪♪

4 5 5 5 5

5 5 4 5 5

3 3 5 5 4 4

4 3 5 4 3 5

5 5 3 3 4 4

7 4 3 3 5 (+2)

7 4 7 5 (+1)

5 7 3 3 4 (+2)

5 3 4 7 5

5 5 7 4 3

The Tuplets
INTRODUCTION

Welcome to the world of quintuplets, septuplets, and so on.

 **You are leaving the world of pop music!**

I only recommend practicing the next couple of pages if you have really worked through (and become comfortable with) with all the previous material.

Now, if you want to drive yourself crazy, here's something for you. When you've mastered the binary and ternary systems in this book and/or the DVD, this stuff will keep you busy. Up until now I chose to keep the focus on material that is very practical and useful right away in the world of Western music: rock/pop/jazz/funk and so on.

But in closing this book I want to give you a "quick start" method to uncode ALL possible patterns, such as the kind found in most complex Zappa-esque music, and Indian and Arabic rhythmic systems.

Are you still there? Do you really want to get into this?

Are you sure?

OK!

If you want to immerse yourself in the world of quintuplets, septuplets, and so on, we have to break the practical letters down into their true basic models.

Twos and Threes:

A five, then, would be 2+3 or 3+2. When I use it in the words chapter, I chose the most common forms of fives and sevens, remember? Five was 2+3, and seven was 2+2+3. You can continue to just use those phrasings for quintuplets and septuplets.

But if you want to have an easy way to build all the possible phrasings, here are the building blocks that you need:

DATE:	TEMPOS:

And of couse our ternary letters:

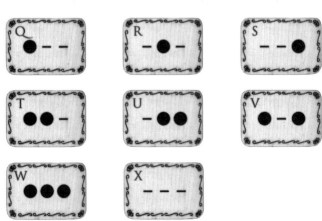

QUINTUPLETS

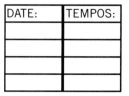

Quintuplets: Now, if you want to put together all phrases in five, you need all the possible combinations of the twos and threes. You should end up with 32 phrases, and here they are:

SEPTUPLETS / NINETUPLETS

Septuplets:

For septuplets, we don't have to find all possible 2+2 combinations because they are all there already in the binary letters. So we simply combine A-P with Q-X but in septuplet subdivision, and you should end up with 128 phrases.

And if that's not enough for you...

Ninetuplets:

You could do the same thing with ninetuplets as well. Combine 3+3+3.
The easiest way here would be to take the letters Q-X in all possible combinations—but I will leave that to you. I think you get the concept by now!

Next, you can do different things, such as:

1. Stay in the tuplet subdivision and go through the snare drum and rudiment chapters using the accents to embellish them with rudiments, or applying all possible stickings to them (again using the building blocks of the letters).

2. See these phrases as groupings over 16th or triplet subdivision, and use them in the exercises of the words and syntax chapters.

3. Apply these groupings like we did the words in the Linear Language chapter.

4. Use the tuplet phrases as fills in the Words Recap Sheets in the words chapter (pages 62,63,64) to get used to the change of subdivisions (WARNING! Don't do this in a ballad on a pop gig!).

5. Take some time off: you are officially crazy!

As a bonus I have something special for you. I get asked a lot about the the solo in the song "Greb Fruit" on the DVD, so here is a complete transcription from the wonderful Mark Eeftens, who wrote out the entire solo for you in great detail (even the falling splash is in there!). Have fun with this.

"Greb Fruit" Drum Solo Key

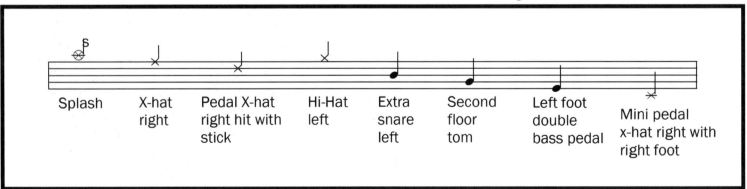

"Greb Fruit" Drum Solo

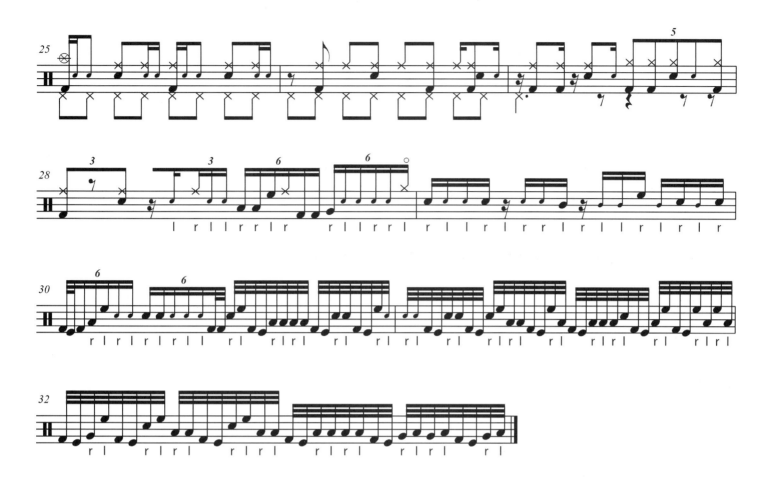

Conclusion

I really enjoyed sharing this material with you, and I hope it takes your drumming and understanding of rhythm to a higher level. Thank you for checking out this book, and letting me spend this time with you as a coach through these exercises.

I hope that this is a book that you can use over and over again, and that the ideas are still useful to you many years from now. I myself go back to these exercises regularly to see if I'm still in touch with the fundamental Rhythmic Alphabet and its applications.

Finding Your Own Voice

Don't be afraid to make full use of the material presented here. Remember: You don't have to reinvent music. Just find your own voice: focus on your individual "*how* to do it," and don't simply stop at "*what* to do." Some musicians try so hard to reinvent music that it's like trying to fight an invisible man.

Practice consciously, let ideas flow and use your repertoire.

Focus on "saying things in your own words." When someone asks you to do that, does it mean that you have to invent words that have never been heard before? Of course not! That would be ridiculous—and simply useless if you want to communicate. We have common ground in language, and that's the beauty of it. We want to hear words we know; the uniqueness comes from the content and message—your feelings—and especially *how* and *why* you say things. No one criticized Shakespeare for lack of creativity because he didn't invent new words, or Goethe for being boring because he used the same letters as everyone else. Whether it is philosophy, literature, or comedy—or for that matter any style of music—the expression of one's character is what it's all about.

And this leads us to the most powerful element of any language; whether it's body language, spoken word, written word, or music:

I'm talking about honesty.

Not only the honesty of the content that you are willing to communicate, but also the honesty of your willingness to communicate! When musicians don't care whether their audience has the chance of following them or not, that's when music loses its traditional purpose and its potential power.

You have to give something that is valuable to others in order to be successful in any field.

So get to know your vocabulary, listen, develop your own voice, be aware of what you want to say, and then share it with other people. If you do that, there will always be an audience.

I can't wait to hear you play one day.

I wish you all the best, and hope to meet you on the road someplace soon.

Benny Greb

CD Track List

01	**Guide Track:** Binary Letters Exercise - slow
02	**Guide Track:** Binary Letters Exercise - fast
03	**Guide Track:** Ternary Letters Exercise - slow
04	**Guide Track:** Ternary Letters Exercise - fast
05	**Call-and-Response Letters:** Binary (1-Bar Call, 1-Bar Response) slow
06	**Call-and-Response Letters:** Binary (1-Bar Call, 1-Bar Response) fast
07	**Call-and-Response Letters:** Ternary (1-Bar Call, 1-Bar Response) slow
08	**Call-and-Response Letters:** Ternary (1-Bar Call, 1-Bar Response) fast
09	**Call-and-Response:** Words (1-Bar Call, 1-Bar Response) slow
10	**Call-and-Response:** Words (1-Bar Call, 1-Bar Response) fast
11	**Call-and-Response:** Words (2-Bar Call, 2-Bar Response) slow
12	**Call-and-Response:** Words (2-Bar Call, 2-Bar Response) fast
13	**Guide Track:** Words Recap Sheet #1 - slow
14	**Guide Track:** Words Recap Sheet #1 - fast
15	**Guide Track:** Words Recap Sheet #2 - slow
16	**Guide Track:** Words Recap Sheet #2 - fast
17	**Guide Track:** Words Recap Sheet #3 - slow
18	**Guide Track:** Words Recap Sheet #3 - fast
19	**JAM TRACK:** Words Recap Sheet #1 - slow
20	**JAM TRACK:** Words Recap Sheet #1 - medium
21	**JAM TRACK:** Words Recap Sheet #1 - fast
22	**JAM TRACK:** Words Recap Sheet #2 - slow
23	**JAM TRACK:** Words Recap Sheet #2 - medium
24	**JAM TRACK:** Words Recap Sheet #3 - slow
25	**JAM TRACK:** Words Recap Sheet #3 - medium
26	**JAM TRACK:** Words Recap Sheet #3 - fast
27	**Call-and-Response Binary Combinations** (1-Bar Call, 1-Bar Response) slow
28	**Call-and-Response Binary Combinations** (1-Bar Call, 1-Bar Response) fast
29	**Call-and-Response Binary Combinations** (2-Bar Call, 2-Bar Response) slow
30	**Call-and-Response Binary Combinations** (2-Bar Call, 2-Bar Response) fast
31	**Call-and-Response Ternary Combinations** (1-Bar Call, 1-Bar Response) slow
32	**Call-and-Response Ternary Combinations** (1-Bar Call, 1-Bar Response) fast
33	**Call-and-Response Ternary Combinations** (2-Bar Call, 2-Bar Response) slow
34	**Call-and-Response Ternary Combinations** (2-Bar Call, 2-Bar Response) fast
35	**Guide Track:** Syntax, Binary - slow
36	**Guide Track:** Syntax, Binary - fast
37	**Guide Track:** Syntax, Ternary - slow
38	**Guide Track:** Syntax, Ternary - fast
39	**Guide Track:** Syntax Revisited, Binary - slow
40	**Guide Track:** Syntax Revisited, Binary - fast
41	**Guide Track:** Syntax Revisited, Ternary - slow
42	**Guide Track:** Syntax Revisited, Ternary - fast
43	**Warm-up to Burnout / Binary Letters** - slow (60-90 bpm)
44	**Warm-up to Burnout / Binary letters** - medium (100 -140 bpm)
45	**Warm-up to Burnout / Binary Letters** - fast (150-180 bpm)
46	**Warm-up to Burnout / Ternary Letters** - slow (60-100 bpm)
47	**Warm-up to Burnout / Ternary Letters** - medium (110-140 bpm)
48	**Warm-up to Burnout / Ternary Letters** - fast (150-200 bpm)

Notes

Notes

Acknowledgments

Benny would like to thank:

All the Grebs and Franks.

Rob Wallis, Paul Siegel, and all at Hudson Music.

Joe Bergamini and Rick Gratton for their great help in getting this book to see the light of day.

Tom Mayer for his incredible artwork.

Norbert Saemann, Udo Heubeck, and all at Meinl.

Thomas Barth, Karl Heinz Menzel, and all at Sonor Drums.

Marco Soccoli and all at Pro Mark and Puresound Snare Wires.

Matt Connors, Remo Belli, and all at Remo.

Stephan Haenisch and all at Hardcase.

And additional thanks to my friend Gerhard Kühne for his constant help, advice, and creativity.

This book is dedicated to my beloved son.

Benny uses:

Sonor Drums

Meinl Cymbals

Remo Drumheads

Pro Mark Sticks

Puresound Snarewires

Hardcase

bennygreb.com